# Passaconaway's Realm

# Passaconaway's Realm

## CAPTAIN JOHN EVANS
## AND THE EXPLORATION OF
## MOUNT WASHINGTON

RUSSELL M. LAWSON

UNIVERSITY PRESS OF NEW ENGLAND

Hanover and London

University Press of New England, Hanover, NH 03755
Printed in the United States of America

5   4   3   2   1

Library of Congress Cataloging-in-Publication Data
Lawson, Russell M., 1957–
Passaconaway's realm : Captain John Evans and the exploration of
Mount Washington / Russell M. Lawson.
p.   cm.
Includes bibliographical references and index.
ISBN 1-58465-167-9 (alk. paper)
1. Evans, John, b. 1730 or 1.   2. White Mountains (N.H. and
Me.)—Discovery and exploration.   3. White Mountains (N.H. and
Me.)—Description and travel.   4. Washington, Mount (N.H.)—Discovery
and exploration.   5. Explorers—White Mountains (N.H. and
Me.)—Biography.   6. Mountaineers—White Mountains (N.H. and
Me.)—Biography.   7. Pioneers—White Mountains (N.H. and
Me.)—Biography.   8. Frontier and pioneer life—White Mountains (N.H.
and Me.)   9. White Mountains (N.H. and Me.)—Biography.   I. Title.
F41.44 .L39 2002
974.2'203—dc21
2002004935

*FOR POOH*

# Contents

# "Daunting Terrible"

This book is about mystery. It is a story of the journey from the valley of the self, of time, to the summit of the transcendent of self and of time. Reason and science are in constant pursuit of the unexplainable, the mystical, the ephemeral, the divine, even as rationalists and scientists try in their futile fashion to discount the transcendent, to make concrete the unknown, to form laws that ignore the spiritual, to provide nomenclature for the unnameable. Humans are forever drawn from the nightmarish reality of everyday life—of war, disease, conflict, death, anguish, fear—to the truth that exists in the unfathomable, the unapproachable, where the mists and clouds, the storms of existence lie far below—and one stands in blazing sunlight next to the heavens. And one *knows*.

Walter Neal, Darby Field, Thomas Gorges, Richard Vines, John Josselyn, Captain Wells, Governor John Wentworth, Nicholas Austin, Captain John Evans, Jeremy Belknap, Manasseh Cutler, Daniel Little, Joseph Whipple, John Bartlett, and Dudley Hubbard—the lives evoked in this book—were the first mountain climbers in the history of North America. Climbing mountains during the seventeenth and eighteenth centuries was something of a new activity among humans. Unlike today, when mountaineering has become the narcissistic pursuit of danger for its own sake, those few who ascended American peaks before 1800 retained a certain humility, an awe before the vastness of the creation, combined with a sense of utility, the confidence that such ascents would yield vital information about geology, landscape, flora and fauna, meteorological conditions, and history. Mountains were standoffish before 1800, an elusive, forbidding, mysterious realm of the divine.

Ancient Europeans, assuming that the most terrible and distant gods had no better place to pitch a tent than on the cloud-covered peak, were content to reside in valleys and worship the abode of the gods from afar. Mount Olympus was a realm forbidden to man. Random shepherds and hunters might traverse less imposing peaks, but great mountains refused to accommodate their human counterparts, heroes such as Odysseus and Jason. Exceptions were generals leading organized troops into mountainous terrain for military and strategic purposes. Alexander the Great, for example, negotiated the Taurus and Hindu Kush ranges of eastern Turkey and Afghanistan. Hannibal of Carthage led an army through the Alps in 218 B.C. The Roman historian Titus Livius recorded in his *History* the Macedonian king Philip V's ascent of a peak in the Hebrus Mountains of Thrace. Philip, according to Livy, thought it made good strategic sense to ascend peaks that could provide him with an extensive vision of the lands and peoples he hoped to conquer. Neither Alexander, Hannibal, nor Philip ventured upon mountains because of religion, curiosity, or personal challenge. Ancient European mountaineering, such as it was, focused on practical military achievements in a realm that was otherwise forbidden, unapproachable, unknown.

The ancient Near East, the homeland of great world religions, naturally had a different tradition than the more secular West. The *Epic of Gilgamesh* tells of the Mesopotamian hero Gilgamesh and his friend Enkidu finding beauty and the divine in mountain regions during the third millennium B.C. On the track of the monster Humbaba, Gilgamesh ascends a mountain and prays for guidance in its divine presence. Likewise the Old Testament indicates that Hebrew patriarchs and prophets such as Abraham and Moses found religious enlightenment atop mountains—Moses was completely changed by his experience on Mount Sinai. Jesus of Nazareth, like earlier prophets, wandered, taught, meditated, and became transfigured upon the mountains of Palestine. That Jesus, the *word*, spent many sublime moments atop mountains indicated for his contemporary and future disciples the spiritual significance of the mountain.

Not until the Renaissance of the fourteenth century, however, do we find Europeans who climbed mountains in search of such exhilarating religious experiences. Reading Livy's account of King Philip's journey inspired in the Italian orator and poet Francesco Petrarca the desire to ascend a neighboring mountain, Mount Ventoux in eastern France, in 1336. The experience of the summit yielded in Petrarch astonishment, reflection, humility, and personal spiritual reformation.

Subsequent mountaineers journeyed to great heights for inspiration but also for knowledge. The wonder and beauty of mountains inspired the Swiss Protestant Conrad Gesner to climb Mount Pilatus in 1555. Gesner, a scientist, believed as did many of his contemporaries that the acquisition of knowledge required active penetration into the unknown. Followers of the reformers Luther and Calvin welcomed the light that science shed on God's works. At the same time the more secular-minded engaged in scientific exploration. Hernando Cortés wrote his sovereign Emperor Charles V in the early 1520s that on two separate occasions he had sent conquistadors to attempt the ascent of Popocatepetl for the sake of discovering the origins and nature of its volcanic activity. Yet notwithstanding the growing interest in natural history, expeditions to mountains during subsequent centuries remained rare.

That mountaineering was the exception rather than the rule during the Renaissance and Enlightenment made the fourteen ascents from 1632 to 1804 of Mount Washington, the dominant peak of the White Mountains and the tallest mountain in the northeastern United States, all the more remarkable. The dozens of men who followed explorers such as Darby Field and John Evans to the White Mountains sought the supposed riches of the mountains: botanical specimens; meteorologic, geographic, and geologic data; personal adventure; and the divine. The best-documented and most exciting of these

journeys was the Belknap/Cutler expedition of 1784, led by
Captain John Evans.

The frontiersman Evans (1731–1807) led men of science
who were also clergymen. Pious scientists were as intrigued
as their secular, deist counterparts with the heights of nature.
The search to know the White Mountains of central New
Hampshire was, as Petrarch knew, a search into the past to
know oneself, to discover one's origins. The explorer felt in
nature divinity, and felt it in himself too. This association of
one personal force with another, this recognition of a mirror
of oneself in nature and vice versa necessarily drew the
seeker—the religious seeker of self, the active seeker of God,
the explorer of natural and personal frontiers—thither to
mountaintops in search of the God of nature that, it was felt
and sensed, is also the God of self: the creator of the massive
peak is ironically, illogically, the creator of the insignificant
individual human. Such a search involves two different types
of seeking, one driven by primal, intuitive urges that are found
in nature and self, the other driven by a more intellectual im-
pulse toward analytical, conceptual answers. Philosophers and
historians usually consider these two realms of searching separate, though they are sometimes merged by organized religion
and natural theology. Jeremy Belknap (1744–1798), who organized the 1784 expedition to the White Mountains, was a
clergyman-scientist, a natural theologian. Belknap went to the
White Mountains seeking to analyze, measure, and collect
useful data; he returned filled with astonishment at the romantic sublimity of the peaks. His friend the Reverend Manasseh Cutler (1742–1817), a scientist and a rationalist, was
able successfully to distance himself from the awesome spectacle that surrounded him. Meanwhile their "pilot" Captain
John Evans, an uneducated frontiersman, interacted with the
environment more by instinct than intellect.

The story of Captain John Evans, the most successful
mountaineer of his time, who blazed a trail up Mount Washington twice, in 1774 and in 1784, is buried deep in the annals
of the northern New England past. One has to dig and imagine

to recreate his life and times and his journeys to Mount Washington, the second of which found him at the head of the first scientific expedition to the White Mountains. Like so many other unheralded frontier guides, axe-men, and hunters, Evans' story is more harrowing and fascinating than those whom he led, the better-known journal keepers and reporters, men such as Jeremy Belknap and Manasseh Cutler. These newcomers entered into what was to them an unknown realm. It was, however, a familiar region to the frontiersman Evans, who had journeyed to the upper Saco valley in 1763 as one of the first settlers of Fryeburg, Maine, making his living carving trails and roads in the wilderness, hunting and trapping, and fighting threatening beasts of the forest and of the mind. John Evans was enough of a historian and thinker to separate himself, intellectually, from the object of his pursuit of a living: the northern frontier, forest, and mountains. Yet Evans lived the wilderness; he was the verge of civilization entering into the unknown. Emotionally and spiritually he was completely tied to, dependent upon, the wilderness, which gave him a different perspective, separated him from his counterparts the natural theologian Belknap and the scientist Cutler.

# Passaconaway's Realm

# Chapter One

# PASSACONAWAY'S REALM

The wind blows from the north. Ceaseless. Endless. The wind bares everything; nothing escapes its power. Its razor edge knifes across hill and dale, scours the surface of rocky peaks that jut into the void of blue, cuts deep into the soil and rock. Battling futility, life tries to escape the blistering cold. Shelves of rock become home to minuscule creatures, lichens and mosses, shrubs with haggard berries, evergreens contorted into shapes that challenge one's imagination—ugly, perhaps, almost absurd, yet alive, hence beautiful.

Spirits of the dead ride the wind where no human dares tread. Chocorua, wailing in desperate anger and anguish over the senseless deaths of his wife and child, over happiness brought to an end, and over his own crime as well, soars, a wind-rider, over the sharp peak, his namesake Mount Chocorua. Kancamagus haunts river valleys where once he and his children hunted and fished—now no more. The greatest rider of the wind is Passaconaway, whose spirit the Penacooks know ascended the Great Mountain, Agiocochook, in a huge bloody chariot hitched to a team of wolves, rising ever higher along the descending rivers, beyond the line of trees, into the dense fog, the ubiquitous cloud cover, the searing cold: he is invisible yet apparent, leaving a trail of death and destruction, warning all who dare journey to the summit of their awful fate, retribution for the crimes of the English settlers, the invaders.

The native peoples—the Penacooks, Sokokis, Ossipees, and Pequawkets of the Saco, Androscoggin, and Pemigewasset rivers—who lived in sight of "the place of the Great Spirit of the forest," Agiocochook, were in awe of the mountain and its

noisy spirits, in awe of Passaconaway; they humbled themselves before his power and refused to ascend the mountain,
preferring to live on the bounty that cascaded from above. The
Sokokis lived in the shadow of the mountain on a high grassy
plateau fed by mountain streams, next to a crystal pond, the
product of enterprising beavers. Theirs was the repetitious existence of men mending tools and weapons, women squatting
over cookholes boiling fish or pounding maize with wooden
mortars, children playing at war. During the winter they lived
in wigwams fashioned from white birch; men hunted using
snowshoes to quicken their pace through the deep snow. The
mountain was their constant companion, ubiquitous like the
sky, sometimes changing appearance but never departing.
They lived and died next to the mountain. But the Sokokis
rarely penetrated its vast wilderness, rarely came to know it
other than from a distance. Such knowledge awaited the coming of others. Downstream from the Sokokis—following the
raging torrent of the Ellis River south to the Saco River—lived
the Pequawkets, who fished the waters of the Saco using weirs
at the falls to catch salmon, hunted bear and deer, and employed simple but effective traps—called culheags—to snare
beaver, marten, and mink. Their preferred mode of travel was
by water, using wonderfully light and buoyant canoes constructed from a cedar, spruce, or maple frame upon which
women used black spruce roots to sew white birch bark for
the shell. Nearby, tribes fished Ossipee Pond and Lake Winnipesaukee from their canoes at night using knots dipped in
pitch and then set ablaze to attract lamprey, bass, pike, pickerel, and salmon. Across the divide on the Pemigewasset and
the Merrimack, other rivers flowing south from the White
Mountains, lived the Penacooks, Passaconaway's tribe. They
dominated the land of what would one day be New Hampshire. Enemies surrounded them, the Mohawks to the west,
the Penobscots to the east, and the Tarrantines beyond that.
A greater enemy, one of penetrating subtlety yet pervasive and
persevering, came from across the sea.

The Atlantic was the highway by which they came in mast

ships with billowing sails, following the winds and currents north along the coast of the New World until they arrived at the sandy shores of New Hampshire and the rocky cliffs of Maine. Giovanni da Verrazano, skimming the cold waters in his ship *Dauphine* in 1524, saw mountains inland of a misty, cloudy whiteness; one peak stood out like a bold cloud on the horizon. Subsequent explorers such as the Frenchman Samuel de Champlain in 1605 saw the mountain gleaming in the distance. The Englishman Christopher Levett, exploring at the mouth of the Saco River in 1624, reported from his conversations with the Indians that "this river . . . cometh from a great mountain called the Christall Hill, being, as they say, 100 miles in the country." Sailors hungering for land after their long voyage, still scores of miles from the coast, sought the mountain standing alone, a seamark, a friendly beacon signaling safe harbors on the horizon.

After many years as a warrior and colonizer, Captain John Smith adopted the roles of fisherman, explorer, geographer, and cartographer in 1614. Smith coasted the cool, midsummer Atlantic waters from Maine to Massachusetts. He sailed in a small pinnace amid the rocky indentations of the Maine coast, along the sandy shores of New Hampshire, past likely harbors and hazardous shoals. He felt the churning of river water as it competed with ocean brine, the Penobscot, Kennebec, and Piscataqua dumping fresh water far beyond their respective mouths. Smith interviewed the native Algonquin tribes, heard of their wars and leaders, their bravery and exploits, and of the inland land, its plenty, its possibility. Smith sailed up the Kennebec fifty miles to see for himself what the land could produce. The plentiful crops and good lives of the Indians impresed Smith. He described the moose and other astonishing creatures. He scanned the distant horizon and used the bearings of his compass to map the landscape. Smith's map of the land that he christened "New England" includes the outline of a mountain inland from Casco Bay. Smith called it Shooter's Hill on the map; in his *Description of New England* (1616) he used the Algonquin name Aucocisco. On clear days, when the haze and fog of summer cleared in the wake of fresh inland breezes, the peak dazzled with the reflection of the bright sunlight. Smith, impressed, declared "the twinkling mountaine of Aucocisco" one of "the chiefe mountaines" of New England. Aucocisco, twinkled, as it were, with crystal and perhaps other gems in the otherwise incredulous mind of Captain John Smith.

Explorers such as Smith made up the vanguard of settlers, seeking fertile land for planting, marshland for grazing, navigable rivers for trade, and safe harbors for towns. Thanks in part to Smith's promotional writings such as the *Description of New England*, what began as scattered outposts of fishermen became lively settlements trading in fish, naval stores, lumber, and furs. The English, associating the use of land with its ownership, staked claims and granted proprietorships—but rarely consulted the natives. Legend has it that Passaconaway sold the lands between the Merrimack and Piscataqua rivers to the English, in particular to the English missionary and founder of Exeter, New Hampshire, John Wheelright. Antiquarians looking back on the supposed deed of 1629 applauded Passaconaway as a *noble savage*, reluctant to give in to the English but helpless not to. Some put great speeches into his mouth wherein he decried his waning power and predicted the victory of the white people in settling the land and making it a bastion of freedom. Others christianized him, making him a willing pupil to the Puritan Apostle John Eliot, even a devout, saintly chieftain to his wayward people. More accurate are tales that he sensed the demographic and military power of the invaders and knew that armed resistance was futile, so he resorted to calling down the anger of the Great Spirit on his foes, those who would clear forests, build fences, dam streams, and bridge rivers. Reputed to be a great shaman, able to metamorphose physical elements and have his way with the spiritual, he failed to turn back the English but established a reputation among his people as a valiant if disillusioned holy man.

Like most prophets, Passaconaway lived to a great age, dy-

*A Glimpse of Mount Washington.* Long before explorers penetrated the northern forests to ascend Mount Washington, the distant peak "twinkled," in Captain John Smith's words, beckoning the courageous to journey thither. *Dartmouth College Library.*

ing only when his prodigious strength vanished in the wake
of hopelessness and despair, worn out recalling lost youth, the
great days of war, victory dances, and plentiful war trophies.
His son Wonnalancet hastened to follow his father's spirit inland, as did all the native tribes, their power and numbers diminished less by war than by disease, their hopes of glory
gone, the mountainous north country beckoning like a refuge
from ignominy. They pursued the journey north, paralleling
descending rivers before gaining the high country, a dangerous
land of uncertain paths, deep snows, and endless forests,
daunting even to the greatest adventurer. In this mountainous
land they heard strange noises, saw shining crystals—the
woods seemed alive and the rivers seemed to speak. If the natives discovered a forbidding environment, it was at the same
time one filled with spirits willing to accommodate the like-
minded but quick to anger when invaders crossed untouched
streams and ascended hills never before trod upon.

The English foothold in the region, meanwhile, centered
upon the Piscataqua River and Great Bay and tributaries—the
Squamscot, Lamprey, Oyster, Cocheco, Back, and Salmon Falls
rivers. The two proprietors of northern New England, Ferdinando Gorges and John Mason, representing the Council of
New England, which had ultimate control of the region, sent
adventurers and settlers to act on the men's behalf; they were
to settle the wilderness, discover the means of production and
profit, and establish as a working financial concern what
Gorges and Mason christened Laconia. It would take men and
women rather like the ancient Greek Spartans to settle the
region, which consisted, according to the historian of New
Hampshire Jeremy Belknap, of "all the lands between the rivers Merrimack and Sagadehock, extending back to the great
lakes and river of Canada." To the proprietors and their hired
adventurers, this land was but a terra incognita, completely
unknown. The "river of Canada" was, perhaps, the St.
Lawrence. The "great lakes," however, were largely lakes of
the imagination, the dominant one of which was purportedly
the Lake of the Iroquois, perhaps Lake Champlain, perhaps

nonexistent. This did not prevent the proprietors Gorges and Mason from giving specific orders to their agents in America to explore the hinterland and discover the lake. Captain Walter Neal, one of several men put in charge of Laconia, arrived on the *Warwick* in March 1630 and took up residence at Little Harbor in the neighborhood of Portsmouth on the Piscataqua River. Neal's associates included Ambrose Gibbins, Richard Vines, and Henry Josselyn. Their goal was the founding of a viable province built upon the fur trade in the region of the Lake of the Iroquois and the river of Canada. Ferdinando Gorges had hoped that war with France during the 1620s would result in the English conquest of New France and control of the fur trade. Peace with France in 1630 ended that hope, which spurred Gorges to encroach upon the fur trade indirectly, using northern New England as a base from which a lucrative trade extending a hundred miles into the interior could develop. The inland wilderness was thought to be pleasant enough; according to Belknap "it was described as containing divers lakes, and extending back to a great lake and river in the country of the Iroquois. This river was said to be fair and large, containing many fruitful islands; the air pure and salubrious; the country pleasant, having some high hills; full of goodly forests, fair valleys and fertile plains; abounding in corn, vines, chestnuts, walnuts, and many other sorts of fruit; the rivers well stored with fish, and environed with goodly meadows and full of timber-trees. In the great lake, were said to be four islands, full of pleasant woods and meadows, having great store of stags, fallow-deer, elks, roe-bucks, beavers and other game, and these islands were supposed to be commodiously situated for habitation and traffic, in the midst of a fine lake, abounding with the most delicate fish."

Captain Neal stayed for three years, from 1630 to 1633, during which time he set up a fortified site, surveyed the Piscataqua valley to form initial township sites, made journeys into the interior in search of precious stones, the river of Canada, and the Lake of the Iroquois, and established a fur trade with the native inhabitants. In 1658, Thomas Gorges, grandson and

heir of Ferdinando Gorges, published a fragmentary yet sug-
gestive account of Neal's journey to the interior wilderness.
"The way over land" wrote Gorges, to the Lake of the Iroquois
"hath been attempted by Captain Walter Neale, once governor, at the charges of my grandfather, Captain Mason, and
some merchants of London, and the discovery wanted one
day's journey of finishing, because their victuals were spent,
which, for want of horses they were enforced to carry, with
their arms and their clothes, upon their backs; they intended
to make a settlement for trade by pinnaces upon said lake,
which they reckon to be about ninety or one hundred miles"
from the "Plantation of Pascataway." Along the way Neal and
his companions discovered "christall stones," which they took
the trouble to lug back to the plantation at the mouth of the
Piscataqua River. Gorges' story convinced Richard Arthur
Preston that Neal discovered "great mountain barriers" that
"stood between New England and the interior of the continent." Neal sent the "christall stones" to London, where John
Mason had the best experts examine them—they turned out
to be worthless.

Did the "christall stones" come from the "chrystall hills"?
Jeremy Belknap spent years before and during the War for Independence researching and writing his magnum opus, the
*History of New Hampshire* (1784). Belknap was especially interested in the history of White Mountains exploration. He
accumulated what was for the time an extensive collection of
data on past journeys to the White Mountains and ascents of
the Great Mountain Agiocochook. Belknap thought that "as
Neal had positive orders to discover the lakes, and tarried but
three years in the country, employing great part of his time in
searching the woods, it is probable" that he did indeed explore
the White Mountains, in the process discovering "something
resembling crystal." Belknap learned, however, that contemporary observers such as John Winthrop (in his *Journal*) and
Reverend William Hubbard (in his *General History of New
England*) claimed that one Darby Field in 1642, rather than

Walter Neal in 1632, was the first to journey to the White Mountains and to ascend the Great Mountain. Belknap knew about Darby Field, but he believed that the adventurer *accompanied* Walter Neal, along with another of Ferdinando Gorges' agents, Henry Josselyn, to the White Mountains. Belknap chose to base his description of the supposed Neal/Field/Josselyn journey on Thomas Gorges and John Josselyn rather than Winthrop or Hubbard. Winthrop recorded that Field went with "divers" others; Belknap assumed the others were Henry Josselyn, the ultimate source of his brother John Josselyn's account, and Captain Neal, as described by Gorges. Belknap was not entirely convinced that Josselyn's description of the journey to the White Hill in *New-Englands Rarities Discovered* (1672) was that of an eyewitness. Somehow he grew to believe that Henry Josselyn journeyed to the mountain and passed on the information to John. In a letter to Governor John Wentworth of March 15, 1774, Belknap wrote: "There is an ancient book extant by one Josselyn, who was somehow connected with Mason, giving some account of the country; if that could be procured, I believe it would be useful." Belknap stated that he was going to Boston to borrow the book as well as look at the many papers preserved by his old friend and mentor Thomas Prince. Prince's papers were subsequently scattered during the War for Independence. Belknap, who was an antiquarian adept at foraging for hidden documents in trunks, attics, and on dusty shelves, discovered a source in Prince's papers—since lost—that convinced him that Henry Josselyn and Captain Neal journeyed together. Neal departed in 1633. Belknap knew from Winthrop that Field journeyed with "others." Hence he assumed that historians such as Hubbard made a mistake in assigning the date 1642 to Field's journey. "But as Neal," Belknap wrote in a note in the *History of New-Hampshire*, "had positive orders to discover the lakes, and tarried but three years in the country, it is probable that Mr. Hubbard mistook one figure in his date," which therefore should read 1632.

Clearly *someone* at some point between 1632 and 1642 journeyed to the White Mountains and ascended the Great Mountain Agiocochook. But who?

Sometime between 1780 and 1784, Jeremy Belknap sat at his desk in the parsonage at Dover, New Hampshire, marshaled all of his sources describing journeys to the White Mountains, and penned "Several Accounts of the White Mountains." He used the remaining pages of a journal book in which years before he had recorded his 1774 journey to the Connecticut River valley to attend the third commencement at the young Dartmouth College. "Several Accounts of the White Mountains" has apparently gone unnoticed among antiquarians and inquisitive others until now. Belknap transcribed seven accounts of journeys to and descriptions of the White Mountains ranging from the first, the Neal/Field/Josselyn journey of 1632, to the last, General John Sullivan's description of the mountains in a 1780 letter to François Marbois.

Examining Belknap's first entry and comparing it to the narrative accounts of Governor Winthop and William Hubbard, it is clear that there are at least three, and perhaps four, separate accounts of independent journeys to the White Mountains undertaken during the 1630s and 1640s. Hubbard condensed his narrative from three different accounts, all derived from Governor Winthrop's *Journal*. Winthrop described Darby Field's first journey, probably in 1642, to the White Mountains, during which two Indians accompanied him. Shortly after his return Field journeyed again to the mountains in the company of "five or six others." Then, at some point soon after Field's return from this second journey, "others" made separate journeys, in particular two men, "magistrates of Sir Ferdinand Gorge[s] his province" of Maine, Thomas Gorges and Richard Vines, who reached the mountains and ascended the highest peak.

Governor John Winthrop heard about Darby Field's 1642 ascent of the Great Mountain from the clergyman Samuel Danforth's almanac for 1647, in which was the laconic entry:

"1642. 4 The first discovery of the great mountaine (called Chrystall Hills) to the *N. W.* by Darby Feild [sic]." Winthrop also found out more about the journey either directly from Field or more probably from someone who conversed with Field—perhaps Thomas Gorges, who described the journey in a 1642 letter to his cousin Ferdinando Gorges. Thomas Gorges wrote:

This much I certify of accordinge as it was sent to me by him that discovered them whose name was Darby Feild of pascataqua who about a month since with some 3 or 4 Indians undertook the voyage, went first to Pigwackett, a place on the Saco river accordinge to my draught now 23 leagues from Mr. vines his house hence he travailled some 80 miles as he sayeth & came to a mountain, went over it, & a 2d & a 3d, at length came to a ledge of rocks which he conceaved to be 12 miles high, very steep, uppon which he travailed going to a rocke that was at the end of that which he judged 2 miles high, very steep, yet he adventured up, but one Indian accompaynge him, the most being fearfull. At the top it was not above 20 foot square, wher he sate with much fear some 5 hours time the clouds passing under him makinge a terrible noyse against the mountains. Thence he discovered some 80 miles farther a very (*glorious*) white mountain & between 2 other great mountains as he judged some 100 miles a mighty river bearing North & by East from him of which like or sea he could see noe end. On this mountain, he mett with terrible freesing weather and, as I took it, on the top of the ledge or rocke & at the foot of them were 2 litle ponds, 1 of a curious red colour, the other black. The [latter] dyed his handkerchief very blacke, the former did not alter the collours. Ther wer many rattle snakes but he receaved noe harm.*

Winthrop recorded his version of the story in his *Journal.* Winthrop called Field "an Irishman," but he could well have been from a small town on the North Sea shore of England. Field probably was part of the Great Migration of English men and women to Massachusetts Bay during the 1630s. The theory that he migrated for religious reasons is supported by his apparent emigration north to New Hampshire in 1638, following the Puritan outcast John Wheelright to the falls of the Squamscott River and the new town of Exeter. He scratched

*Quoted in Laura and Guy Waterman, *Forest and Crag: A History of Hiking, Trail Blazing, and Adventure in the Northeast Mountains*, Boston: Appalachian Mountain Club, 1989, 12.

his mark next to his name in 1639 along with other residents of "Piscataquacke"—the Piscataqua valley—declaring their intention, as "brethren of the church of Exeter," to live with "wholsome lawes & government" that were "agreeable to the will of god" and submitting to "our Dread Soveraigne Charles [I]." He was present in 1638 when the "Sagamore of Piscataquacke," Wehanownowit, granted "all the right, title and interest in all such lands woods meadows rivers brookes springs as of right belongs unto me from Merrimack River to the Patents of Piscatoquake," as well as in 1639 when the same Indian granted "for goode consideration all the meadows and grounds extending for the space of one English mile on the east side of Oyster river." Field found Oyster River, a beautiful stream that rises and falls with the tide and flows into the Great Bay, sufficiently attractive to move his wife and children, around 1640, to the neighborhood, where he set up business selling spirits. Possibly he was, like Walter Neal before him, employed by Ferdinando Gorges. He seems to have resided at Durham Point, a peninsula that juts into the Bay a few miles north of Exeter.

Precious emeralds and crystal stones, rather than more mundane material goods such as furs and trade, lured Darby Field to the White Mountains. English settlers of the seacoast such as Field learned from the native inhabitants to hold the mountains in awe as places of mystery and danger but also incalculable wealth for those brave enough to make the journey. Field set out alone, but not from Oyster River or any of the tributaries of the Piscataqua, which would have forced a long overland journey already shown by other adventurers, including perhaps Captain Neal, to be unfeasible. Rather Field journeyed north along the coast by foot or boat to Saco River, which he ascended by canoe. The English learned quickly that Algonquin birch bark canoes were best suited for river travel; Field likely traded with local natives to acquire his canoe. Winthrop wrote that Field's journey lasted eighteen days, the first few spent ascending the Saco, finding portage around the several falls. Field had reported that the journey from the mouth of the Saco to the mountains was one hundred miles, an accurate estimate as the crow flies. By canoe, he discovered, it is much longer; the river winds tediously in and out, carving massive intervales along the shore. Unending forests of pine, maple, oak, beech, and birch surrounded the river. Field ascended past the Little Ossipee River, the Great Ossipee River, and the Cold River flowing south from the mountains before finally reaching the Ellis River, which flowed from the eastern slope of the Great Mountain. It was up this eastern branch of the Saco that Field journeyed until he arrived at "an Indian town of some 200 people"—the Sokokis tribe. There two adventurous tribesmen conquered their initial fears—death was said to be the result should they go where no Indian had previously journeyed—and joined Field for the ascent. Perhaps Field, similarly superstitious although monotheistic, convinced the natives that the wonders of the mountain were material rather than spiritual in nature. Perhaps the natives, having used the mountain on a daily basis to gauge bearings in the forest, decided to come to know it better. These three adventurers journeyed up a ridge between two great gulfs on the eastern slope, discovering snow on the mountain even though it was June. "[Near] the top was neither tree nor grass, but low savins, which they went upon the top of sometimes, but a continual ascent upon rocks." They were engulfed in clouds that broke once they ascended above the tree line to the shrubby, rocky peak. During the ascent they discovered "two ponds, one a blackish water and the other reddish." Once they reached the initial summit they spied the rocky height that leads to the highest summit, upon which was a "plain about 60 feet square. On the north side there was such a precipice, as they could scarce discern to the bottom. They had neither cloud nor wind on the top, and moderate heat. All the country about . . . seemed a level, except here and there a hill rising above the rest, but far beneath them." Field "saw to the north a great water which he judged to be about 100 miles broad, but could see no land beyond it. The sea by Saco seemed as if it had been within 20 miles. He saw also a sea to the eastward, which he judged to be the gulf of Canada: he saw some great waters in parts to the westward, which he judged to be the great lake [of the Iroquois] which Canada river comes out of. He found there much muscovy glass," a form of talc, of which he and his companions "could rive out pieces of 40 feet long and 7 or 8 broad." Winthrop does not say but one assumes that Field returned to the seacoast by the same route, descending Saco River.

Darby Field's second ascent of the Great Mountain, information about which Governor Winthrop undoubtedly acquired from the same source as the first, occurred "about a month after." Field this time "went . . . with five or six in his company," which could mean either five or six acquaintances, or five or six men who were like him (perhaps) active in Gorges' Laconia operation. Winthrop's *Journal* indicates nothing about his route or its length. Assuming this journey took place in July, the men probably did not encounter any snow; they did experience "some wind on the top, and some clouds above them which hid the sun"—in other words it was frigid on the summit. We now hear for the first time from Winthrop the motive of these two journeys in the space of a month or two: "They brought some stones which they supposed had been diamonds, but they were most crystal." Likewise Walter Neal a few years earlier had acquired from some unidentified location crystal that he took to be diamonds only to find out they were beautiful yet worthless. Was Field acting in the wake of accounts circulating among the Laconia adventurers of Walter Neal's similar pursuit of the supposed fabulous wealth hidden on the summit of Agiocochook?

Winthrop provided, in addition to the two accounts of Field's journeys, a narrative of another journey, apparently taken in October of the same year. Thomas Gorges and Richard Vines were the only two men Winthrop mentioned among "divers others" who became mountaineers in the wake of Darby Field's "report . . . of shining stones." The apparent cause and effect relationship implied in Winthrop's story is not altogether clear. Long before Field's journey the English had heard tales of the mountain's wealth in crystal, shining stones, and carbuncles, that is, shining gems—the mountain's glimmering, "twinkling" whiteness suggested as much. Perhaps these "divers others" journeyed after Field's much-publicized return, or perhaps they were part of a host of adventurers who sought the wealth of the mountains both *before* and *after* Field's return.

Richard Vines and Thomas Gorges were officials in Ferdinando Gorges' Maine proprietorship. Vines, according to Belknap, journeyed to northern New England at the request of Ferdinando Gorges, perhaps first in 1609, then later in 1616; Vines captained a ship that set to fishing while he explored the coast, trading with and learning about the native Algonquins. At the time, the Indians were enduring a terrible pestilence because of which large numbers died. Yet "Vines and several others" tarried "in the country through the winter, lived among [the Indians] and lodged in their cabins, without receiving the least injury in their health." Vines was a magistrate as well as an early settler of Saco, Maine, founded at the mouth of the Saco River and hence in the direct line of travel for adventurers and traders seeking the wealth of the White Mountains. Saco was the capitol, as it were, of Gorges' hopeful province of New Somersetshire; Vines became his chief representative, the deputy governor, of the province (soon to be called Maine) in 1639 along with Thomas Gorges, Sir Ferdinando's cousin. The two essentially ruled the province jointly for the next few years (and explored it together as well) until Thomas Gorges departed for England in 1643.

The journey of Vines and Gorges to the mountains lasted a fortnight. They set out from the town of Saco and ascended the river "in birch canoes" to the "Indian town" of "Pegwagget." The journey to Pequawket by river was ninety miles; they either assumed or heard from some earlier traveler that the overland distance to the town was but sixty miles. The explorers had to find portage for ten falls that hindered the navigation of the Saco. From Pequawket they ascended "30 miles in woody lands," paralleling the Ellis River to the east

slope of the Great Mountain, which they then ascended. At
the first summit they discovered "a plain about 3 or 4 miles
over . . . and upon that is another rock or spire, about a mile
in height, and about an acre of ground at the top." On the
initial summit, the plain, they thought they had discovered
the origin of the grand rivers of northern New England; Winthrop argued that they were looking at the origin of the Saco,
the Androscoggin, the Kennebeck, and the Connecticut. The
western slope of the mountain gives rise to the Saco as well
as the Ammonoosuc, a tributary of the Connecticut. From its
eastern slope originates the Peabody, a tributary of the Androscoggin. The Kennebeck, however, rises in Maine. The
highest peaks of the White Mountains, the two adventurers
further discovered, run east and west for thirty to forty miles.

In sum, Winthrop's *Journal* provides three accounts of journeys to the White Mountains, all during the same year, and
alludes to other journeys to the mountains at about the same
time. These are the three accounts that historians have long
used to try to reconstruct these trips. Samuel Danforth and
Thomas Gorges provided independent collaboration that
Darby Field did indeed journey to the White Mountains in
1642. Belknap, however, discovered another account of uncertain origin that he transcribed in his manuscript journal "Several Accounts of the White Mountains." Belknap followed
William Hubbard, who had in turn followed Winthrop, but
about a quarter of the account is entirely new information not
found in any hitherto known source. It reads:

1642—or rather 1632. In the summer Captain Neal, Mr. Joselyn with
Darby Field and others travelled to the White Mountains. They
passed through many of the lower and rainy clouds and ascended to
the top. There is a plain 60 feet square on the top, and a very steep
rising on the west side *so as there was no clambering up without
holding fast of the brush growing on the sides of it. The waters continually running down the sides of it from above. On the top of the
hill is a pond of water wherein some of them waded being about
knee deep.* All the country about them which is a ridge of hills
seemed to them level land. There was great expectation of precious
stones to be found there *by the glistening of some white stones.*

Something was found like chrystal but of little value. These hills give rise to several great Rivers.

The italics here denote those words found in this account that do not come from the other printed sources—Hubbard's *History* or Winthrop's *Journal*. In the italicized parts, there are a few passages that are particularly noteworthy and bear the marks of direct experience. The descriptions of waters running down the sides of the mountain and of the need to hold on to the evergreen shrubs that dominate the mountain above the tree line could well have been constructed using Winthrop's *Journal*. However, in neither Winthrop's nor Hubbard's accounts of Darby Field and Richard Vines is there mention of a pond of water on the summit. John Josselyn's *New-Englands Rarities Discovered*, published in 1672 and purporting to describe a journey to the Great Mountain during the 1660s, does describe a pond on the summit. Belknap transcribed Josselyn's account on the next page of "Several Accounts of the White Mountains," showing that the information about the pond for the Neal/Field journey derived from a source other than Josselyn. Most important is the minor detail of men wading up to their knees in the pond, which is sufficiently concrete to be clearly based on an eyewitness. Who was that eyewitness?

Belknap has been justly criticized for making several errors of judgment in the description of the Neal/Field/Josselyn journey in the *History of New-Hampshire*. He ironically used John Josselyn's account to describe Darby Field's journey. He clearly confused John and Henry Josselyn: John visited his brother Henry, who was an agent of Ferdinando Gorges in Maine, in 1638, but he was not in New England in 1632 nor in 1642. Henry Josselyn could have been in New England in 1632; early documents of his whereabouts are unclear. When Belknap composed this section of his *History of New-Hampshire* before the Revolution, about 1774 or 1775, he was either unaware that there were two brothers Josselyn, or he assumed that Henry joined Neal and Field on their 1632 journey to the mountains and passed on information of the journey to his brother John, who recorded it in his book. By the time Belknap transcribed "Several Accounts of the White Mountains," he was aware that there were two Josselyns—he prefaced his transcription from John Josselyn's *Rarities* with the note: "He was brother to the other Joselyn," meaning Henry. Belknap transcribed the "Several Accounts of the White Mountains" at some point between 1780 and 1784 as a preface, as it were, to his own journey at the end of July 1784. But even as late as 1792, when Belknap reissued volume one of the *History of New-Hampshire*, he still believed that Josselyn's account in *Rarities* related to the journey of Neal, Field, and Henry Josselyn in 1632.

Notwithstanding the confusion of Belknap's published and manuscript accounts of the first journey to the White Mountains, we are nevertheless left with a tantalizing narrative of journeyers—perhaps Walter Neal, perhaps Darby Field, perhaps Henry Josselyn, perhaps others—who ascended the Great Mountain, Mount Washington, as early as 1632, who discovered a pond of cold water on the summit, who waded in the water up to their knees, to the tops of their boots, and who returned to tell their tale to someone, though exactly who remains uncertain. The antiquarian manuscript hunter Jeremy Belknap got his hands on the account but did not cite the source. Belknap used the account along with Thomas Gorges' *America Painted to the Life* (1658) to construct his narrative of the Neal/Field/Josselyn journey in the *History of New-Hampshire*. Belknap believed that the three explorers journeyed on foot, shouldering their supplies, hiking into the heart of Laconia until the dense forests and impenetrable mountains—as well as the vision of never-ending wilderness from the summit of the Great Mountain—forced their return.

Henry Josselyn, at the time that Thomas Gorges and Richard Vines made their ascent of the Great Mountain, was a magistrate who had been in Maine for almost ten years, serving as the "steward," or agent, of John Mason and Ferdinando Gorges. Belknap thought that Henry Josselyn joined Neal and Field on their 1632 journey. Though this was probably not the case, could Josselyn have been one of the "divers others" who, according to Winthrop, journeyed to the White Mountains? That at some point between the 1630s and the 1660s Henry Josselyn ascended the Great Mountain is made less dubious by the presence of his brother John Josselyn's account of a journey to "one stately mountain . . . surmounting the rest."

It was natural for John Josselyn to journey to and write about the White Mountains. Josselyn, who was born about the same time that John Smith christened New England, lived most of his life in England, practicing medicine. But like others before and since, he thought of America as the ultimate source of *materia medica*; hence he voyaged to New England to visit his brother Henry in 1638 and again during the 1660s. Late in life he described his journeys and the wonders of America in two separate books, *New-Englands Rarities Discovered* (1672) and *An Account of Two Voyages to New-England* (1674). Like most contemporary scientists Josselyn was not an empiricist, rather an Aristotelian intent on collecting, describing, and cataloging the varieties of flora and fauna. His interest in botany grew out of the practice of medicine. Early modern scientists were always in search of antidotes, purgatives, and analgesics. Henry Josselyn, having spent time with the Algonquins of New England, would have learned of their varied potions and remedies. We can imagine Henry writing to John of the veritable cornucopia of medical information to be garnered from travels and studies in New England, which would have resulted in John's two voyages thither. John discovered on his journeys along the New England coast, up rivers and into the interior forests and mountains, communicating with native inhabitants as well as with English settlers, what worked for toothache, what antidotes there were for snakebites, how to settle an upset stomach, how to reduce fever, what to take to rid oneself of the kidney stone, and what relieved the swelling and pain of gout. Folklore, common sense, and home remedies went a long way toward health and happiness according to John Josselyn.

Josselyn's search for *materia medica* took him to the White

Mountains, where he apparently ascended, during his second voyage to America, the Great Mountain. His account, found in *New-Englands Rarities Discovered*, appears to be that of an eyewitness. Even so, Josselyn did not record the names of his companions or any details of the journey. He did provide an accurate portrait of the White Mountain wilderness. As Belknap transcribed the account in his "Several Accounts of the White Mountains":

Fourscore miles NW of Scarborough a ridge of mountains runs NW and NE one hundred leagues known by the name of the White Mountains, upon which snow lieth all the year and is a landmark 20 miles off at sea. It is a rising ground from the sea shore to these hills and they are inaccessible but by the gullies which the dissolved snow hath made. In these gullies grow saven bushes which being taken hold of are a good help to the climbing discoverer. Upon the top of the highest of these mountains is a large level or plain of a days journey over whereon nothing grows but moss. At the farther end of this plain is another hill called the sugar loaf, to outward appearance a rude heap of massive stones piled one upon another and you may as you ascend step from one stone to another like a pair of stairs, but winding still till you come to the top which will take half a day and yet is not above a mile where there is also a level of about an acre with a pond of clear water in the midst which you may hear run down, but how it ascends is a mystery. From this rocky hill you may see the whole country round about. It is far above the lower clouds and from hence we beheld a vapor like a great pillar drawn up by the sun-beams out of a great lake or pond into the air where it was formed into a cloud. The country beyond these hills northward is daunting terrible being full of rocky hills as thick as mole hills in a meadow and clothed with infinite thick woods.

Josselyn, providing further observations in *Two Voyages to New-England*, wrote that "the Countrie within [New England is] rockie and mountainous, full of tall wood, one stately mountain there is surmounting the rest, about four score mile from the Sea." The fertile valleys amid the mountains have great plenty "of goodly Trees," "grass," "spacious lakes," and "ponds well stored with Fish and Beavers." The White Mountains are "the original of all the great Rivers in the Countrie"; their peaks "are richly furnished with mines of Lead, Silver, Copper, Tin, and divers sorts of minerals, branching out even to their summits, where in small Crannies you may meet with threds of perfect silver." Josselyn knew enough about the White Mountains to refer to them as an almanac for predicting the weather: "If the white hills look clear and conspicuous, it is a sign of fair weather; if black and cloudy, of rain; if yellow, it is a certain sign of snow shortly to ensue." He accurately described the pesky "black fly no bigger than a flea, so numerous up in the Countrey, that a man cannot draw his breath, but he will suck of them in."

Passaconaway's realm of the White Mountains was left to the beasts of body and mind for many years after Josselyn's travels, during which time those rare journeys undertaken into the "daunting terrible" remoteness of wilderness were for political and military reasons. A boundary dispute in 1652 led two explorers, John Sherman, a soldier, and Jonathan Ince, a Harvard College student, to follow the Merrimack upriver from its mouth at Newburyport, Massachusetts, into New Hampshire to its source at Lake Winnipesaukee in the shadow of mountains to the north. King Philip's War twenty years later again forced colonials northward. In December 1676, a company of soldiers pursued the Indians north of Ossipee Pond into a region where they "discovered nothing but frozen ponds and snowy mountains."

Subsequent years of war between the English and French spilled over into regional conflicts involving the colonists of New England and the colonists of New France and their Indian allies, the Penacook and Sokokis tribes of the upper Connecticut, Pemigewasset, Androscoggin, and Saco rivers. The Indians living at Pequawket, later Fryeburg, Maine, found themselves directly in the path of sporadic, ranging companies of Massachusetts and New Hampshire soldiers intent on revenge and scalps. French-instigated Indian attacks on Maine, New Hampshire, and Massachusetts settlements during King William's War, which began in 1689, brought terror and reprisals. Companies of soldiers typically pursued the enemy into the deep woods and mountainous regions of New Hampshire and Maine. Major Jeremiah Swaine wrote his superiors in October 1689 that the "chestnut woods" along the Cocheco and Oyster

rivers turned up none of the enemy, so he thought it "advis-
able to send a considerable party to Ossape and Pigwaquit,
white hills &c." The itinerant natives, constantly on the
move, were more elusive than the settled colonists, who were
easy prey for the attackers. Often the invaders took captives
north to Quebec through the woods, up traces paralleling rivers through the notches of the White Mountains. Hence many
English settlers were unwilling explorers of the White Mountains; some died en route due to, as Belknap described it, the
"hardships of travelling half naked and barefoot through path-
less deserts, over craggy mountains and deep swamps, through
frost, rain and snow, exposed by day and night to the inclem-
ency of the weather, and in summer to the venomous stings
of those numberless insects with which the woods abound; the
restless anxiety of mind, the retrospect of past scenes of pleasure, the remembrance of distant friends, the bereavements
experienced at the beginning or during the progress of the captivity, and the daily apprehension of death either by famine or
the savage enemy."

Warfare during Queen Anne's War (1703–1712) and Dummer's War (1722–1725) continued to bring many rangers to the
mountain wilderness, particularly to Pequawket because it
served as a rendezvous point for raiders and because it was
favorably situated on the line of trade and travel from the upper Connecticut to the Saco River. The spring and summer of
1725 were particularly active in this regard. The provinces of
New Hampshire and Massachusetts offered a bounty of one
hundred pounds to scouts and rangers willing to brave the wilderness and return with Indian scalps. Both provinces had effective militia programs that trained men who were used to
wilderness travel and privation, knew how to handle weapons,
and felt sufficient hatred and desire for revenge to search out
and destroy the enemy. Captains from Massachusetts and New
Hampshire led teams of men up the rivers descending from
the mountains in hopes of discovering Indians and taking
home trophies for the reward. From September to October
1725 Captain Samuel Willard led a ranging party from the Pe-

migewasset River northeast to the Swift River, then to the
Saco River, halting finally at Pequawket, which had lately become infamous due to the bloody battle waged between Captain John Lovewell and the Pequawket Indians. Lovewell, of
Dunstable, Massachusetts, and his men, having had success
killing Indians during the winter, returned in May 1725,
marching north of Lake Winnipesaukee to Ossipee Pond,
where they built a fort and left a garrison. Lovewell and thirty-
three men then continued north to the Saco and Pequawket.
At what became known as Lovewell's Pond, the rangers met
a party of native raiders led by the Pequawket chief Paugus
who, according to legend, was a giant and a great warrior. A
violent and bloody contest ensued during which Lovewell and
a dozen of his men fell.

At the same time another ranger captain, John Gyles, got
to know the mountains well by leading scouts in and about
the Saco, Androscoggin, and Ammonoosuc rivers. Gyles had
once been a captive of the Abenakis of the Penobscot region,
from whom he learned of the attempts of native mountaineers
to climb the "White Hills" of the upper Penobscot called
Teddon (now Mount Katahdin), only to fail because of the presence of ghostly "Spirits" who apparently made a few adventurous natives "strangely disordered & delirious." Notwithstanding Gyles' journey of April 1725 up the Androscoggin
River to the New Hampshire White Mountains, he maintained
years later in his *Memoirs* (1736): "The White Hills called Teddon at the head of Penobscot River are by the Indians said to
be much higher than those called Agiokochook above Saco."
Impressed, Belknap transcribed Gyle's claims in "Several Accounts of the White Mountains."

Generally the rangers and scouts of 1725 who journeyed
among the rivers and valleys of the White Mountains found
not the enemy but rather the silent and sublime mountain
forest. In volume three of the *History of New-Hampshire*,
Belknap tells of the only recorded ascent of the Great Mountain during all of these wars, the only one since Josselyn's of
perhaps sixty years before, and the only one for another fifty

years to come. "A ranging company, who ascended the highest
mountain, on the N.W. part, April 29th, 1725, found the snow
four feet deep on that side; the summit was almost bare of
snow, though covered with white frost and ice, and a small
pond of water, near the top, was hard frozen." The rangers
remain otherwise unidentified in Belknap's *History*, and he did
not discuss their motives, which must have been a bit unusual
for rangers—they could hardly have expected to find scalps on
the mountain! Simple fascination may have been reason
enough for their ascent.

Fortunately, Belknap provided more information, if only for
himself, in his manuscript "Several Accounts of the White
Mountains." Here we find out that one Captain Wells led the
party not on April 29 but on April 18. Belknap's transcription
from an unknown source follows:

The white mountains run in a range N.E. and S.W. We went up to
the top. Saw Amariscoggin River on the other side running down
from the N.E. under the range and with a southern bend, then bearing
away S.E. from us. We also saw another water to the N. about 12
miles off which we supose to be Coneticut R. Ammenoosuck River
runs down a great descent from its very head near 90 miles to its
entering Coneticut River. The mountains rise pretty sloping for 2 or
3 miles and then exceeding steep to the top. About a mile from the
head of the river we first met with snow on the back or N.W. side,
exceeding hard and grew deeper even to 4 feet near the top. But the
top appeared to be pretty bare of snow tho' covered with thick white
frost and ice among the moss and small bushes but about 6 inches
high there being no tree or higher bushes thereon. The whole top
seemed to be a rock with a very little mosy sort of earth with it—so
thin that we could easily kick off bushes and all with our feet and
discover the rock which appeared to be a whitish grey with a good
deal of Ising-glass intermixed. On the top was a pond hard frozen,
about 4 or 5 rod broad and 6 or 7 long and tho' it was a clear still
warm sun shining day and but noon yet here we found it so very cold
that we could hardly endure it and therefore quickly marched down
again to the Westward. We set our compass on the top and found
Winepiseokee bearing S. 6° W.

Captain Wells led his scouts from the northwest side of the
Great Mountain, the first recorded ascent from that direction.
They apparently journeyed along the Ammonoosuc River to
the Western (now Crawford) Notch. Like Gorges and Vines,

Wells discovered the talc "ising-glass" on the summit, as well as the pond atop Josselyn's Sugar Loaf. Had they the desire to wade in the pond up to their knees, they could not because of the ice. They descended the mountain the way they had come.

One wonders whether or not William Douglass saw the same source that Belknap used. Douglass, in his *A Summary, Historical and Political, of the First Planting, Progressive Improvements, and Present State of the British Settlements in North-America*, published in 1760, discussed the "remarkable mountains." He concluded that their whiteness derived "not from their being continually covered with snow, but because they are bald a-top, producing no trees or brush, and covered with a whitish stone or shingle." It would be difficult to make this conclusion based on Winthrop's account of Darby Field's journey or Josselyn's two narratives of 1672 and 1674. Only Captain Wells describes the "whitish grey" stones of the summit. Who was Captain Wells? Belknap's transcription bears the marks of having received it directly rather than having read it from a book. Did Belknap know and communicate with an elderly Captain Wells?

The conclusion of Dummer's War brought a temporary end to hostilities in New England. The natives gave up their desperate attempt to defend and preserve their homeland and receded farther north, making the St. Francis River of southern Quebec the center of future military activity. Meanwhile the seacoast settlements grew, the commerce of Portsmouth expanded, and settlers journeyed further inland in search of fertile land, mast trees, and furs. But few traveled by land beyond Ossipee Pond and Mount Chocorua; few canoed the Saco beyond the falls to Pequawket. Few penetrated the notches, those natural furrows amid the great peaks. The White Mountains yet remained elusive, unconquered, a vast symbol of timelessness and peace.

*Chapter Two*

# THE NORTHERN FOREST

The decade of the 1740s was an age of intrepid men and heroic deeds. Such was the young Jeremy Belknap's perception of the year of his birth, 1744, when King George's War, the Cape Breton War, began. For Belknap as for all New Englanders the smell of the sea was ubiquitous, its draw unending; the sea was the great route of the Atlantic, the source of food and fortune, danger and death—and the highway for French ships coursing from the north, intent on plunder and destruction. The war began as did most wars of the eighteenth century, over minor local politics combined with grand international strategy. Upon hearing that war in Europe had begun again, French troops struck the English garrison on Cape Breton, an island off the coast of Nova Scotia; they took control of the island and fortified it at the fortress of Louisburg. This inspired New Englanders led by William Pepperrell of Maine to attack the fort, an ill-advised, apparently foolhardy maneuver that brilliantly succeeded. Meanwhile more mundane yet equally lethal conflicts dominated the mountainous frontiers of New England. Settlers by 1740 had journeyed further inland following the Connecticut, Merrimack, Lamprey, and Cocheco rivers. Although much of the action occurred on the Connecticut, involving attacks on Fort Number Four in Charlestown, New Hampshire, rangers and scouts were also sent out to the upper rivers and mountainous areas in search of the enemy, as in earlier conflicts.

Walter Bryent of Newmarket was an experienced surveyor who journeyed north of the Salmon Falls River into the forests east of Lake Winnipesaukee in March 1741 to determine the

Maine/New Hampshire line. It was spring, and the rivers were thawing, hence crossings were uncertain. Indians halted Bryent north of Ossipee Pond, answered some of his inquiries about the hills to the north, but wondered about his intentions, intimidating him sufficiently that he dared not continue. War on the frontiers in late winter 1747 brought Bryent back, this time as a scout for a ranging party. He penetrated the White Mountains and at one point, hearing gunfire in the distance, thought he had discovered the enemy. Upon investigation, the gunfire turned out to be noise caused by "the falling of huge stones from a mountain that hung over, the snow being now melting and the frost coming out of the ground." Belknap interviewed Bryent in 1774, when the former was journeying westward and the latter lived at Suncook. Bryent told the historian that "he also observed smoke to rise, as they thought, which on examination proved to be a cloud or fog driving through a high perpindicular fissure in a rocky hill which looked as if it had been split by an earthquake." Bryent, like Captain Wells before him, had journeyed toward the Western Notch. Although he did not ascend the Great Mountain, he observed that "the western sloping [side is] easy of ascent," which Belknap declared "a mistake," as "the only practicable ascent is on the eastern side." But this was in 1774, before Belknap had the benefit of reading Captain Wells' account.

Bryent and his men could find none of the enemy, though they were nevertheless about, as seen by the raids on varied frontier towns such as Gorham, Maine, from which the Indians took captives through the mountains to Quebec just weeks after Bryent's scout in the Western Notch. Raiders attacked farmers, men and boys, in a field at Rochester, New Hampshire, in June 1747; "three lads," including one George Place, were instrumental in discovering the enemy and driving off the attackers. The preceding autumn raiders had similarly intended an ambush of worshippers at the meeting-house at Penacook, New Hampshire, "but, seeing some of them go armed to meeting, were afraid." The next morning the raiders accomplished their purpose, notwithstanding that Penacook was a fortified town, ambushing and killing five men.

Such was the childhood memory of John Evans. A native of Woburn, Massachusetts, Evans' family, John's father David and mother Abigail, were settlers who journeyed from Massachusetts when the lands about Penacook became open for settlement after Dummer's War. The region of the upper Merrimack River was a favorite place of many veterans of that war, including some who had fought with Lovewell. Penacook, often called Rumford and after 1765 called Concord, was during John Evans' youth a small town of several hundred farmers who worked the fertile intervales formed by the Merrimack. The town served as a garrison, a point on a line of defense against French and Indian incursions. David Evans along with other farmers, including Robert Rogers' father James, performed garrison duties. John's father died during or immediately after the Cape Breton War. His mother remarried Jacob Shute, a former comrade of David Evans, in 1746.

Throughout his life John Evans built his reputation on woodcraft and his abilities as a hunter and trapper, skills that he acquired during his youth roaming the woods in and about Penacook; west toward Mount Kearsarge, which forms part of the watershed from Mount Washington to Mount Ascutney and which towers above the pine forest; north along the Merrimack Valley to the foothills of the White Mountains; perhaps still further north to the Pemigewasset and Baker rivers, where the waters were clear and sweet and the game was abundant. On sunny days the surrounding peaks provided ample inspiration to would-be explorers and discoverers. John would hunt with friends and his younger brother David; they might travel by birch bark canoe upriver or, more likely, take to the woods following deer traces or old Indian paths, using snowshoes in winter and moccasins in summer, carrying furs, traps, and supplies on wooden sleds. They would dress in buckskin, carrying ammunition on belts, their rifles held in their arms or slung on their shoulders, feeling their skinning knives at their sides.

When not hunting and working on the farm of his father or stepfather, John worked as a hired hand and farm laborer for, among others, the Reverend Timothy Walker, who served the parish from 1730 to 1782. Walker was a Harvard College–educated preacher who was almost as worldly as his parishioners. He lived well in a large, opulent, two-story house. Involving himself in local politics, he was town leader, teacher, "counsellor," and historian. A practical preacher, he eschewed the theological disputes brought on by the New Light enthusiasm of the Great Awakening and focused instead on Christian behavior. Walker owned land in and about Penacook. Farm hands such as John Evans carted dung, cut down trees and hauled away logs, hewed timber, supervised the burning of brush, plowing of new land, and sewing of seed, constructed fences of wood and stone, mowed grass and "raked hay," carted grain in wagons or dragged it by hand sleds to the mill, and used teams of horses or oxen to drag logs to the mill or retrieve hundreds of "long shingles from the mast swamp." One imagines that, like any hired hand, John Evans often served on one of the many mast teams that would depart Penacook, a center for the mast industry, and venture into the deep woods to select and cut down the towering white pines for use by the British Navy. Such work required all the skills of woodcraft that one could muster: axe-work, working with teams of horses, clearing paths in the forest, hauling off fallen masts, and dragging masts to the Merrimack for shipment to the coast. Mast team members had to know how to prepare a bed of saplings and smaller trees to cushion the crushing force of the falling pine. During summer they had to know how to raise the mast using chains, levers, and pulleys onto a make-do cart with massive wheels and axles. During winter they had to raise the mast onto a sled. When dragging the mast the most difficult operation was always to slow its acceleration on a descent and increase the force of the pull on an ascent.

One anecdote survives time to suggest the relationship of John Evans to Timothy Walker. Walker and Evans one day

went to the fields to work "with a team and cart." Along the
way

they had to pass a very wet and muddy place. In passing it, John sat on
the cart tongue, or neap, while Mr. W. was in the cart. When about
mid-way of the muddy place, John slyly pulled out the pin which held
the cart down, and dropped it, to make Mr. W. think it worked out ac-
cidentally; up went the cart, and out went Mr. Walker into the mud
and water. He got up, and said, "John, this is a bad accident, but drive
on, and I'll go back." A few days after, Mr. Walker having been absent
from home, he went late in the afternoon into the field where John
was at work. When it was time to go home, Mr. W. told John that *he*
would drive the team, and accordingly took his seat on the cart
tongue, while John was in the cart. At about the middle and deepest
part of the muddy place, Mr. Walker pulled out the pin, and down
went John into the mud and water, and was thoroughly soused. When
he got up, Mr. W., holding up the pin, says to him, "John! John! Here
is the pin: *I didn't throw it away!*" A hearty laugh ended the joke.

John Evans was seventeen years old when peace arrived in
New England with the Treaty of Utrecht in 1748, which ended
the Cape Breton War; but peace vanished quickly in 1755
when fighting broke out on the western frontier of the Ohio
Valley and the northern frontier of Lake Champlain and the
upper Connecticut River. For five years New Englanders
fought as British citizens against the French and their Indian
allies, the most notorious of whom were the Indians of St.
Francis in lower Quebec. The St. Francis Indians knew convenient portages in the waterways between the St. Francis
River and the Connecticut River on which they descended and
brought terror to the frontier settlements. Companies of New
England soldiers, intent on revenge, marched from Fort Number Four, Fort Dummer, and Fort William Henry in acts of
reconnaissance, subterfuge, and aggression against the French
fortresses of Ticonderoga, which guarded the water route between Lake George and Lake Champlain, and Crown Point,
which controlled the navigation of Lake Champlain and protected the route to New France. New Hampshirites such as
John Evans, typically inured to danger and fatigue, expert at
stalking and marksmanship, and used to bivouacking in the
forest and living off its scanty produce, became natural re-

cruits for ranger companies raised for the traditional purpose
of seeking out and destroying the enemy. Evans' friends William Stark, John Stark, and Robert Rogers were commanders
of such companies, which were organized by order of the British Crown. Evans himself served under Lieutenant John Stark
in 1759 when the British and Americans, under the leadership
of General Jeffrey Amherst, captured Ticonderoga and Crown
Point. In August Stark and his men, numbering two hundred,
built a wilderness road from Crown Point southeast through
Vermont to Fort Number Four. Rangers such as John Evans,
hacking through dense forests and finding their way amid the
gorges winding about the Green Mountains, became expert
wilderness road builders. It took Evans and his fellow rangers
less than a month to construct what must have been a very
primitive road—a trail in the wilderness to allow unimpeded
troop movements. By mid-September they were back at Crown
Point, awaiting further orders.

Now that Crown Point was secure, General Amherst, an-
swering to years of fear and frustration and the desperate urge
for vengeance against the Indian raiders of St. Francis, ordered
Major Robert Rogers to lead his companies of rangers north,
stealthily, to attack and hopefully wipe out the St. Francis Indians and end their decades-long threat. Local tradition has it
that John Evans as well as his brother David were sergeants
under Captains John and William Stark and Major Rogers.
About two hundred rangers departed Crown Point, rowing
boats that hugged the shore, to the northern extreme of Lake
Champlain. Their attempt to escape detection by the French
failed, but Rogers pursued the advance north through swampy,
boggy spruce forests; the men slept in trees by night. Illness
and happenstance reduced their numbers to 142 rangers, who
exited the "spruce swamp" the first week in October. The men
linked their arms, forming a human bridge, to cross the rapid
St. Francis River. Rogers and two rangers reconnoitered the
Indian town, which they discovered to be engaged in festive
dancing. The rangers struck just before sunrise. Rogers guessed
that they killed at least two hundred men, women, and chil-

dren. Dawn brought with it, in Belknap's words, "a horrid scene; and an edge was given to the fury of the assailants by the sight of several hundred scalps of their countrymen, elevated on poles, and waving in the air." The rangers suffered few casualties but knew that their luck would not hold unless they quickly ascended the St. Francis and then took to forest trails past Lake Memphremagog to the Connecticut River. They rapidly advanced, taking what little food they could muster—which was not much. A few rangers gathered booty rather than food. Some fools dragged along a ten-pound silver statue of the Virgin Mary and silver candlesticks stolen from the altar of the St. Francis mission church. Pursued by French and Indians, they journeyed in a southerly direction as a group for ten days before splitting up into small bands of men so as to evade the enemy more efficiently as well as forage for food. The former was more plentiful than the latter, which consisted of little more than roots, mushrooms, and tree bark—whatever game inhabited these parts fled either the armies of men or the cold weather that made the men's hunger more miserable. David Evans later claimed that hunger forced him and his men into cannibalism, but even this was an insufficient repast. John Evans recalled living off mushrooms and roots for about a month, during which time they became ad hoc road builders by utter necessity. Food was, according to prior arrangement, supposed to await the wandering bands of rangers at the junction of the Connecticut and Ammonoosuc rivers. But the hungry men who survived that long found nothing. The hardy and persevering, such as John and David Evans, continued on. John led a company of perhaps twenty-five men to what was called the Cohos Intervales, rich and fertile land that had not yet been cut by the plow. Hunger drove them down the Connecticut, perhaps by means of a thrown-together raft, until they reached Fort Number Four, in the first week of November, in utter misery and weakness.

The fall of St. Francis, along with the conquest of Quebec, the taking of the fort at St. John, and the fall of Montreal "gave peace to the frontiers of New Hampshire," in Belknap's words, "after a turbulent scene of fifteen years; in which, with very little intermission, they had been distressed by the enemy. Many captives returned to their homes; and friends who had long been separated, embraced each other in peace. The joy was heightened by this consideration, that the country of Canada, being subdued, could no longer be a source of terror and distress." The mountain wilderness and river valleys of the north country were now open for settlement. "The passion for occupying new lands" complemented the Treaty of Paris ending the French-Indian War in 1763.

Residents of Penacook experienced new, domestic conflicts after the fall of Quebec. Evans, who by this time owned a small farm, discovered that his and his neighbors' lands in the town of Penacook, the charter of which was granted by the government of Massachusetts, were the subject of another grant to other settlers by the government of New Hampshire, due to the still uncertain boundaries. Citizens of the town of Bow sought some of the lands of Penacook, including John Evans' farm. Evans and other Penacook citizens sued for the right to maintain the possession of their lands. The issue was too confusing, however, and too close to home for local officials to decide. Timothy Walker, who represented his fellow townspeople in the conflict, journeyed to England three times before the issue was finally arbitrated by the British Crown in 1762. John Evans and other Penacook landowners lost their land.

Simultaneously Colonel Joseph Frye of Andover, Massachusetts, petitioned the province for a grant of land in the district of Maine, at this time controlled by Massachusetts. The government granted Frye proprietary rights over the land of the upper Saco once inhabited by the Pequawket tribe and known by that name though sometimes called Pigwacket. Massachusetts soldiers had long known about the rich intervale lands of Pequawket, and the Peace of Paris presented a wonderful opportunity for settlement. Frye's proprietorship required that he survey the land into lots and grant rights to individual proprietors who would settle the land and build houses and farms.

John Evans was one of the first settlers of the proprietorship, occupying Lot One of the seven lots held by the first inhabitants. Indeed the new town, as yet unincorporated, was known simply as *Seven Lots*. Evans journeyed from Penacook to Pequawket during the summer of 1762 to bring supplies in anticipation of the move. He took familiar paths from Penacook to Rochester, then blazed a trail from Rochester north past Ossipee Pond to Pequawket. Along the way he surveyed the route and marked trees as a precursor to a road. He returned the following summer to cut a path to a proposed mill site at Lovewell's Brook. In November 1763 the thirty-two-year-old Evans brought his wife, Elizabeth, who was two years younger, and their three daughters, aged ten, three, and one. Elizabeth Stickney Evans, a native of Penacook, who had seen her second- and third-born children die a mere nine months apart in 1759, while John was away fighting the French and Indians, put her surviving children in God's hands as she accompanied her husband on this daunting journey. John's unmarried brother David joined them, as did other Penacook emigrants, the families of Samuel Osgood, Jedediah Spring, Nathaniel Merrill, and Moses Ames. They journeyed through falling snow, bivouacking at night under makeshift shelters cut from evergreens. Crossing the rapid and full Ossipee River by horse was difficult on the women and especially the children, who were unaccustomed to such wilderness travel. The men dragged supplies by hand sleds and had to resort to snowshoes the closer they got to Pequawket, at which they arrived in a heavy snowstorm with two feet of snow on the ground.

The first winter at Fryeburg was cold and barren. Several families shared a hunter's cabin; men spent their days on snowshoes hunting for game and trapping; women cared for the children as well as huge kettles of steaming stew. Everyone waited for spring. The Evanses brought seeds for planting; they lay dormant until the thaw and mud of April and May. One imagines Evans on an early spring day in late March, surveying his land. Evans received several parcels of land collectively designated Lot One, as well as the Mill Lot, giving him rights to the first mill built on Lovewell's Brook, which flowed into Lovewell's Pond, also encompassed by his land. Lovewell's Pond in March would still be frozen, with a few patches of water amid the solemn gray ice that heralded the coming warmth of spring, when storms would whip the water white and squalls would make canoeing treacherous. The late winter pond was solitary, still. Soaring white pines surrounded it, a great evergreen fence; during summer months the reflection of the trees in the still water of evening was sublimely beautiful. Peace reigned over the pond in March 1764, but it had not always been this way. Evans, not a scholar but a thinker, inquisitive in his way, particularly about his new lands and their history, knew vaguely of the distant past and Lovewell's Battle at this precise location. Remnants of the Pequawket tribe still inhabited the area. Their village had once been nearby, a little over a mile west of Lovewell's Pond, on the eastern banks of the Saco. Evans got to know these natives, some of whom were with Rogers at the attack on St. Francis. Old Philip was a Pequawket who served as a guide for Rogers and supported the Americans during the Revolution. It was perhaps from him, or someone like him, that Evans heard the Indian side of the story of Lovewell's Battle. His source had been one of the besiegers of Lovewell's desperate force, a native who knew the region, knew that the Pequawkets used the pond for its resources—often they crossed it in canoes—and knew precisely the array of forces that day when Lovewell lost his life.

Through his Indian historical guide, his own observations, and his imagination, Evans could picture the battle. Musket balls whistled through the air, playing sweet music to the brave lads who escaped their fury. Thuds accompanied this music, lethal drums that found their mark in human flesh. Other balls hit surrounding trees or splashed harmlessly into the pond in back of them. The invaders' situation was desperate. Their leader, Captain Lovewell, was one of the first to fall. Surrounded by Indians intent on vengeance, the remaining rangers loaded and fired muskets with a rapidity that few lived to remember. They thought of their wives, their children—and their scalps. But few men this day were to see the setting sun. The Indians bore down on the rangers, who found themselves trapped on a sandy bank at the southwestern edge of a peaceful cove of the pond. In front of the rangers a soggy bog halted their escape. To their right the raging Lovewell's Brook, fed with water from melting snows, was "unfordable." To their left waited the Indians, protected by granite boulders. To their rear was the pond, its icy water as deadly as the musket balls. The rangers' only protection were scattered rocks and pitch pine trees growing near the water's edge.

Evans could still see the marks of the balls on the aged trees. He could faintly make out the names of the dead, carved on the trunks long ago. Visualizing the episode, it astonished him that the rangers could have marched into a region and abandoned their packs on the trail to pursue one lone Indian on the other side of the pond—an open invitation for ambush—without securing the rear. Then to allow themselves to end up in such a "forlorn" situation! More astonishing still was that the Indians quitted the fight upon the arrival of darkness, notwithstanding that they had the rangers "completely in their power." The stories of those who survived and returned to Massachusetts became the stuff of legend.

The environs of the pond were a constant source of supplies for John Evans and his family. He fished the waters for pickerel, perch, and bass, hunted the fowl looking for a place to nest and the animals seeking food and cool waters, gathered shellfish, and laid traps for beaver, lynx, and marten. As Fryeburg grew after the early years of sporadic settlement, Evans had to go farther afield to trap and hunt. His farm supplied basic necessities; pelts, hides, and meat brought a sense of economic security, even wealth. Trapping was hard work with long hours. Winter was the best time to trap. Every day Evans went out to check traps and set new ones. At times he would be gone for days, journeying north to the Androscoggin Valley, hunting in the mountains, following the Saco upstream toward the White Mountains, or passing through the notch later named for himself. Evans Notch traverses forest so dense that the surrounding peaks can be scarcely perceived. Rather like the notch, John Evans himself pierced the highlands, forging paths between lichen-spotted granite boulders, over rotting logs and spongy mats of moss, through solemn stands of white birch trees. That Evans even discovered his notch, blanketed as it was with the verdurous luxury of the virgin forest, reveals that he possessed the attributes of the frontier. He had an intuitive awareness of his place in the whole, a willingness to merge with the natural surroundings. He eschewed the call of science, of reasoned inquiry. Evans was a *natural man*, nakedly human, attired in the culture and customs of the forest.

On the hunt Evans sought the small ponds formed by enterprising beavers at work. Beavers had the knack of using birch branches and mud to dam small streams. These lodges, situated away from the shore, hid a "subterraneous passage" that exited onto land by means of a small hole—the perfect spot to place the scented trap. Evans used steel traps scented with the oil of the beaver to attract the aquatic animal. For other fur-bearing animals—"wolves, bears and martins"—Evans used the Indian trap, the *culheag*. He only needed a sharp hunting knife to construct one. The trapper found two mobile logs of any variety of wood; they had to be of equal length. One log was raised over the other by means of sturdy hickory sticks. One stick held the bait, and the trapper often scented the entire area. When the victim crept into the area and tugged at the bait, the upper log came crashing down on his head, protecting the husky winter coat of fur.

The Maine forest was many things in Evans' time: mud in spring, black flies in June, mosquitoes in August. The rich smell of wildflowers hovered about the humid meadows of summer. Fog hung on the pond, bringing a chill to the air, an eerie, ghost-like presence before the mid-morning sun conquered the shadows. Silence pervaded all. It dangled from trees like moss, surrounded the tall swaying pines, exuded from the forest floor, a padding of rotting leaves, fern, and dried pine needles. On some days the silence was thicker than the fog,

more pervasive than the forest, more daunting than the surrounding peaks. Mount Kearsarge rose to the west above Fryeburg, a visible sign of peace and of danger that precisely reflected the surrounding woods. The mountain blocked the
Fryeburg villager's vision of the north country, of the White
Mountains, of the Great Mountain. Lovewell's Pond did, however, afford a view of the Great Mountain. And Evans ascended
Kearsarge on the hunt often enough to see the mysteries that
lay on the other side. The mountain wilderness beckoned and
tempted, like a siren of the sea: come find what cannot be
found, see what cannot be seen, know what cannot be known.
Test yourself, and know yourself. Journey hither, and return a
different man—*if you return at all.*

Evans always did. He moved strongly through the forest,
silently, mirroring the still environment, as noiseless as a pan-
ther, alert, watching, listening, sniffing the air for signs of
game or danger. He knew instantly by the freshness of the
dung how long it had been since a deer or bear had passed
through the woods. Tracks told him in what direction. Then
he would spy out an old animal trace and pick up the trail like
a bloodhound. Evans gauged directions Indian-style by means
of the growth of moss on trees—always on the north side of
the trunk, away from sunlight. Forced to bivouac at night, he
either constructed a hasty evergreen shelter or merely wrapped
himself in his blanket and slept under the canopy of towering
trees and distant stars; "in foul weather" he would "spread"
his "blanket on sticks, and lie under it." He was confident
from experience, courageous from having endured danger, tire-
less from the many times of privation. His Welsh heritage was
reflected in his blue eyes, thick beard, heavy eyebrows, brown
hair, and silent bearing. On the trail his pace quickened upon
finding familiar trees and meadows, spying the smoke from
the hearth in the distance, seeing familiar fields, barren in
winter, blooming in summer, of maize, surrounded by his own
handiwork, a fence of stone heaped about, a portrait of labor
and sweat, a sign of cultivation and survival. Evans entered a
small rustic cabin, the kettle steaming, tended by his "rib,"

Elizabeth. She was the beautiful and sweet—if only to him—mother of more and more children as the years passed—eleven in all, eight of whom survived beyond childhood. William, their sixth, was born soon after their coming to Pequawket, in April 1765.

Evenings were spent by the fire, performing simple tasks such as cleaning weapons, sharpening blades, mending clothes, polishing pans. The family hearth joined them in treasured moments of simple sharing and love, wordless conversations and knowing glances, frequent stories and gossip, and the ubiquitous tales of the mysterious past. The natives passed along their trepidation about the unknown forest, their fears about the daunting mountain wilderness. Passaconaway loomed above all else, towered above the memories and anxieties of the mountain folk, was present in the echoing thunderstorms, in the crashing freshets of spring, in the unexpected tragedies of frontier living, in the brooding nights when the wind shrieked with his voice. The dreamlike state engendered by the howling north wind could produce in the imagination, heightened with expectation by the tales of the hearth, strange sights and sounds, a moaning coming deep from the forest, a cry for help, a cry for revenge. On rainy nights when the wind fell cool on one's face and the surrounding forest and peaks were enveloped in darkness, glimmers of light might be seen, like a lantern glowing in a harbor fog. Lights and sounds in the credulous mind became guttural, barbaric, inhuman cries accompanied by ghostly figures, perhaps on chariots, the eerie wheels of fire churning in the night, coming closer, becoming brighter, howling and screaming, eyes of burning embers, hypnotizing, terrorizing. Hence did Passaconaway personify the nightmarish unknown of the northern forest.

Even the most intrepid, incredulous frontiersman was subject to the spell cast by the mountain wilderness. Evans' old friends and comrades Robert Rogers and his rangers succumbed to the allure of the Great Mountain, its challenge and possible reward. The most compelling mystery of the Great Mountain during the 1760s—and after—was what happened to those rangers who, driven by greed, carrying the silver image of the Virgin Mary stolen from the St. Francis mission, thought that the White Mountain wilderness might offer them solace from the furies of the dead, and the guilt, that pursued them all along the retreat from the Indian village of St. Francis. After the rangers split up into foraging parties at Lake Memphremagog, this hapless band of nine, apparently lost, found their way to the descending Israel River, which they paralleled upstream to higher elevations. Sensing horrible demons all about, they buried their plunder in a mountain cave, hoping to retrieve it at a later date, to no avail; they succumbed to avenging hunger and cold. All died save one who returned to the settlements of New Hampshire, a man forever changed. Soon after one hunter claimed to have been visited by a spiritual presence in the form of a mission church, burning candles, and a glimmering silver Virgin upon the altar.

When and what precisely drove Robert Rogers to the Great Mountain is unknown. Did he seek redemption in the recovery of the silver Virgin? Was his a penitential journey to the Great Mountain to rid himself of the tortured images of his past? Or was he seeking adventure, another success to tack on to his many other brave deeds? Whatever the reason, Rogers tried to scale the mountain. But the man who seemingly could not be mystified by anything, who had endured the cold, hunger, and fatigue of the march to and from St. Francis, even he could not overcome the challenge of the mountain. The historian Jeremy Belknap, fascinated by Rogers' failure, recorded Rogers' own account of the attempted ascent:

The most considerable mountains in this Province (N Hamp) and indeed in N[ew] E[ngland] are those called the White Mountains, so called from their appearance which is like snow, consisting as is generally supposed of a white flint, from which the reflection of the sun is very brilliant and dazzling, and by their prodigious height are to be seen at a very great distance, being often discovered by the seamen coasting the Eastern shore when all the intermediate land is entirely concealed. It is not known that any person was ever on the top of these mountains. The Indians have often attempted it in vain, by reason of the change of the air they met with which Rogers says he is inclined to believe, having ascended them himself till the alteration of air was very perceptible, when he had not advanced half way up. The valleys below were then concealed by the clouds. Indeed there are several other Mountains in this country whose tops are above the ordinary clouds rarely if ever receiving the benefit of rain upon them. The basis of the White Mountains is a tract of about fifty-five miles square, from which they rise in cragged heads one above another in an irregular manner all they way to the top. For the first 4 or 5 miles of ascent there are found beech, hemlock, and some white pines, higher up the growth is chiefly black spruce for 6 or 7 miles, where the sides are clad with a white moss. Up higher scarce any thing is found growing, for which reason if there was no other the ascent would be very difficult the mountain being extremely steep. There are many streams of water gushing out of the sides which run down with great rapidity; indeed all the largest and best rivers in N[ew] E[ngland] take their rise from some part of these mountains. By all which streams the riches of these hills whose tops are inaccessible are annually carried to and distributed among the neighbouring provinces.

Another Massachusetts native, Daniel Little, the minister of the First Parish of Kennebunk, Maine, could on clear days see the distant summit and hence was similarly taunted by the apparent inaccessibility of the Great Mountain. Soon after his establishment in the ministry, Little wished to journey to the White Mountains and kept a close lookout for potential companions for such an expedition. In 1766, having formed an acquaintance with the new minister of Dover, New Hampshire, Jeremy Belknap, and having discovered the obvious interest in natural history of his new friend—having learned that Belknap, too, spent long moments on clear days wistfully peering at the distant, beckoning peaks—Little proposed that they journey to the White Hills. The Reverend Little formed a plan that involved, it appears, others as well, then wrote Belknap the following letter: "If the Expedition to the White Hills should be prosecuted this Season, whatever news worthy of Notice shall be communicated with Pleasure; if it should be postpon'd to another Season, you may expect to be advertised."

Reverend Little rather than Reverend Belknap appeared to

*Sketch of Jeremy Belknap.* Jeremy Belknap was, among his late-eighteenth-century contemporaries, the chief human and natural historian of the White Mountains. He was as well the organizer of the Belknap/Cutler expedition of 1784. *New Hampshire Historical Society.*

the objective observer more qualified to tackle those distant, rugged peaks. Little was tall and not altogether unimpressive in his bearing; he was as well abrupt and sanguine, impulsive to a fault. His early years were spent in frontier settlements; even now, in 1766, he lived in a gruff fishing town. Rather than feeling a call to join polite society, Little made plans to journey to the east, to the Penobscot and beyond, and rather like an apostle, bring Protestantism to the natives and unlettered settlers in a region once the object of the missionary zeal of French Catholics. Unlike most of his colleagues of the cloth, Little was not an alumnus of Harvard or Yale, his father having determined when Daniel was young that colleges were havens of loose morality. The boy, as a result, had private tutors to inculcate Latin, Greek, even Hebrew. Little developed into a pragmatic scholar who was bored with speculative and dogmatic theology, who preferred an active role within the parish, who took to heart the pastoral office of the clergyman. Little became, as would his new friend Belknap, a Calvinist who tended toward beliefs in universal redemption, more apt to preach about good works than signs of election.

Jeremy Belknap, likewise, enjoyed a reputation for practical benevolence among his friends and parishioners. A native of Boston, Belknap in his early years molded his character and imagination upon the yarns of sailors who loitered about the wharves and rope-walks of Boston harbor awaiting adventure, as did the young Belknap. But the son of a tanner and leather-dresser eventually eschewed the call of the sea for the call of God. He attended Harvard College intent on living up to the expectations of his family on his mother's side, which included the celebrated cleric Mather Byles, to pursue a career as a clergyman. Belknap heard a further call upon graduating, this time from the more earthy, less sophisticated fishing settlements of the Piscataqua. He journeyed to Portsmouth in 1764, then relocated to Dover, a mill town on a tributary of the Piscataqua, the Cocheco, in 1766, becoming the minister of the First Parish the following year.

The history of the Piscataqua region had been formed not

only by fishing and shipbuilding but also by the conquest and harvesting of the forest. The tributaries of the Piscataqua produced mill towns, the economies of which were based on lumber, masts, and naval stores. Such towns, Dover among them, were natural prey to the vengeance and violence of Indian raiders. Belknap arrived to a town with a long, bloody past. The new pastor soon accommodated himself to his surroundings, and like his parishioners molded his fears and expectations on the northern forest, which was not only the source of livelihood but of terror as well. Belknap quickly learned that the townspeople of the frontier settlements of the Piscataqua Valley looked to the northern mountain wilderness as the source of marvelous stories and mystery. Every child knew that the mountains held wonderful crystal treasures that, hidden by the light of day, could be seen shining on unapproachable mountain summits by moonlight. Everyone knew of the terrible fate of the hapless rangers who added the silver Virgin to the quota of hidden treasure of the mountains. Good-wives warned their children never to tread into the northern wilderness for fear of incurring the wrath of Passaconaway. Belknap, trained in the ways of reason and science, eschewed talk of Passaconaway's curse. Yet the stories and mysteries of the White Mountains became an irrevocable source of attraction all the same.

Belknap's entire being turned toward the natural and human past. His mentor in historical inquisition was the great New England antiquarian Thomas Prince, whose *Chronological History of New England* Belknap hoped someday to imitate and to surpass. The past of the Piscataqua and northern frontier became rich fodder upon which Belknap repeatedly grazed. He journeyed throughout the Piscataqua to learn about the region's natural history and talked incessantly with his elders, particularly men like Theodore Atkinson of Portsmouth, who knew so much about, had even participated in, New Hampshire's dynamic and troubled history.

Belknap's interest in the natural and human past of New Hampshire helped to solidify a growing acquaintance with

New Hampshire Provincial Governor John Wentworth. Wentworth was the kind of man Belknap respected and admired. Belknap saw in the governor many of the qualities that he himself lacked; Wentworth was resolute, adventurous, and affable. A graduate of Harvard, son of former Lieutenant Governor John Wentworth and nephew of his predecessor Benning Wentworth, he was wealthy, "in the prime of life, active and enterprising in his disposition, polite and easy in his address." "Though bred a merchant," Belknap recalled in the *History of New-Hampshire*, "he had a taste for agriculture, and entered vigorously into the spirit of cultivation. He frequently traversed the forests; explored the ground for new roads; and began a plantation for himself in the township of Wolfeborough," at the eastern shore of Lake Winnipesaukee. "His example was influential on other landholders," such as the Portsmouth merchant Joseph Whipple, "who also applied themselves in earnest to cultivate the wilderness."

Upon beginning serious research into the New Hampshire past in 1772, Belknap found Governor Wentworth unusually interested in contributing his assistance in garnering sources from others as well as in providing his own observations. Wentworth was uniquely qualified to do both. He had an insider's view of the course of New Hampshire politics over the preceding sixty years. He knew or had known most of the principal politicians and merchants who influenced New Hampshire history during the eighteenth century. But it was not just politics about which Wentworth was well informed. He was also an acute natural historian, was quite expert in botany, and had himself journeyed to the White Mountains in 1772.

In a brief relation of his journey two years later, Wentworth was not clear about the particulars. He apparently approached the Great Range, highlighted by the Great Mountain, from the south, perhaps ascending Saco River to trails that he thought would lead him to the highest peak. He ascended what he believed to be the Great Mountain, but the view from the summit convinced him that another summit to the northeast may well have been higher. Peaks to the southwest of Mount

Washington include Mount Monroe, Mount Franklin, and Mount Pleasant (Eisenhower), any of which Wentworth might have climbed.

Belknap wrote in his *History of New-Hampshire* that the mountain wilderness frequently deceives newcomers respecting mountain heights and distances. This is particularly true of the White Mountains, a massive range covering hundreds of square miles and composed of four dozen significant peaks. The most dominant mountains are the Presidentials, highlighted by Mounts Washington, Adams, Jefferson, Madison, and Monroe, all over five thousand feet. Two significant gaps, or notches, frame the Presidentials, the Eastern (Pinkham) Notch and the Western (Crawford) Notch, through which primitive roads were built before and after the Revolution.

The White Mountains, the highest elevations in the northeast, are part of a grand chain of peaks, the Appalachian Mountains, which forms the eastern divide and watershed of the continental United States. The Indians believed they were "endless mountains"—indeed they stretch a thousand miles from the Carolinas to Maine, characterized by distinctive, much heralded ranges: the Great Smokey, Blue Ridge, Allegheny, Catskills, Berkshire, Adirondack, Green, and White mountains. The Appalachians are the source of all great rivers of the eastern seaboard. They were for two centuries the chief barrier to western settlement, and for an even longer period they remained in places impenetrable and unknown, the habitation of the spirit world, retaining the primordial mark of creation.

Chapter Three

# EVANS OF FRYEBURG

In August 1774, the otherwise sedentary Reverend Jeremy Belknap set out from Dover on a journey west that would take him to the foothills of the White Mountains, inspiring in his mind reflection on the possibility of wilderness exploration. Belknap's intent was to journey to the Lower Cohos Intervales of the upper Connecticut River, then proceed to Hanover to attend the third commencement of the new Dartmouth College. He kept a journal of his travels. Along the way he visited Walter Bryent at Suncook and discussed the "ancient matters" of Penacook history with the Reverend Timothy Walker. From Penacook (Concord) Belknap journeyed north, paralleling the Merrimack and then the Pemigewasset rivers. At Boscawen he "lodged at Capt. Gerrish's but slept not, the bed being preoccupied by innumerable vermin." At Plymouth, a new town situated in the shadows of the White Mountains, Belknap observed that "the river here frequently changes its course and leaves islands and sometimes points of land on one side which belonged to the other, and the old course of the river becomes a pond in the form of a horse shoe." From here, in the company of other gentlemen including the surveyor-general of New Hampshire, Captain Samuel Holland, as well as William Stark, Belknap ascended Baker's River through mountainous country. They passed the spot where, in 1752, William and his brother John were hunting when attacked by raiding Indians. Stark told Belknap he was familiar enough with the mountains to explain the origin of mountain springs, a phenomenon that consistently perplexed mountaineers, who often looked for the hidden source within the bowels of perhaps hollow mountains. Stark claimed that

*A New Map of New Hampshire,* by Jeremy Belknap. Jeremy Belknap's journeys and observations led to this precise engraving, which accompanied volume two of his masterpiece, *The History of New-Hampshire,* 1791. *Dartmouth College Library.*

the mountains have three feet of soft turf that covers "an hard pan of blue earth" that is "impenetrable by water." The soil, like a sponge, is constantly moist and becomes the ongoing source of mountain springs. Belknap thought that Stark's theory was valid when combined with the phenomenon of clouds repeatedly producing moisture. Belknap also thought it reasonable "to suppose that mountains are composed of hard and durable substances, or they could not remain undiminished through ages." Belknap's ruminations and discourse, which appear, in retrospect, elementary, illustrated the opportunities and limitations of eighteenth-century science, which lacked a clear theoretical foundation based in empirical study and had to rely more on "Nature Displayed" supported by a childlike fascination with remarkable phenomena.

At Orford on the Connecticut River the men witnessed just such a remarkable meteorological event. A "large black cloud broke," Belknap recorded in his journal, slammed "against" a mountain, unleashing "a torrent of rain," the moisture of which immediately re-formed into "vapors" that ascended "again in spots from the sides of the mountains like so many small fires about in the woods. These steams soon collected into clouds and furnished other showers which held all night, and the next morning we saw the same process repeated, which was indeed very curious."

In this region, the Lower Cohos, small mountains hem in the meandering of the Connecticut River. The men entertained themselves trying to guess the height of a hill on the other, Vermont, side, then crossed the river to get a closer look. "I found myself much decieved [sic] in the appearance, it proving to be in reality double the height which I supposed, as we judged by a nearer inspection and a comparison of the height of trees both under and upon it." Flowing from the mountain "was a spring of the coldest water I ever tasted."

After the ceremonies at Hanover, on the route home through southern New Hampshire, Belknap had his imagination further stirred by "the Grand Monadnock, which is the highest mountain in these parts and the largest of a very long crooked range of mountains which go by the name of the Pack Monadnocks," meaning *isolated hills*. "On the top of this great mountain is a cramberry [sic] meadow. We could see many bare rocks among the trees." Belknap's friend James Winthrop would in a few years use "a barometer, and the table of corresponding heights, in Martin's *Philosophia Britanica*," to arrive at an estimate of the height of Grand Monadnock at 3,254 feet.

The towns of the Cohos Intervales on the Connecticut River, stretching from Lyme to Orford to Haverhill to Lancaster to Northumberland on the Upper Ammonoosuc River, were home to recent immigrants from western Massachusetts and Connecticut. These Upper Valley towns felt isolated from the settlements of the seacoast, but in 1774, this isolation was about to change. New roads, following old Indian traces, were being built through the notches of the mountains to connect frontier settlements with the markets of the Piscataqua Valley.

The initial instigation to build roads through the mountains came from the inhabitants of Lancaster, Northumberland, and Shelburne, northwest and northeast of the White Mountains. Men of the former settlement, such as Timothy Nash and David Page, recent emigrants of Massachusetts, formed themselves into a "committee" in 1767 "to look out and mark roads to the 'Ameroscoggin,' Pickwackett, and the first settlements on the Connecticut." Governor Wentworth in 1772, frequently journeying to his plantation at Wolfeborough—and further to the White Mountains—ordered Surveyor-General Holland to investigate possible routes for roads in the north country. One route was obvious: Timothy Nash of Lancaster had blazed a trail in 1771 through the Western Notch—a narrow pass through the mountains hitherto unknown to white settlers though long known to the Indians.

Enterprising settlers and land speculators who took advantage of Nash's discovery included Joseph Whipple of Portsmouth. Whipple belonged to one of the old families of New England. Descended on his mother's side from the Cutts, he enjoyed the privileges of wealth and status that came naturally

*Sketch of Joseph Whipple.* Joseph Whipple, who ascended Mount Washington in 1784 and repeatedly examined it from the perspective of his Dartmouth, New Hampshire, plantation, doubted that Mount Washington was the highest summit. *New Hampshire Historical Society.*

to merchants of the Piscataqua. The Whipple family hailed originally from Massachusetts; Joseph's father, however, moved to Kittery, Maine, where Joseph was born in 1738. As a young man he went to sea along with his brother William. By 1760 the two brothers had established a mercantile store at Portsmouth. Joseph was successful in trade as well as in land speculation. The latter, apparently, was the motive behind his decision in 1773 to journey through the Western Notch, where the Saco originates on the western slope of the Great Mountain, to the northern highlands. He found a likely spot amid a small range of mountains that the natives called Waumbekmethna, next to a river called Siwooganock. To Whipple the river was the Israel, named by an area hunter, Israel Glines, in a successful attempt to enter the pages of history. Whipple built a log cabin, planted corn, and brought livestock and servants alike to make his summer home livable and profitable. In time he built a two-story house located on paths to and from the Androscoggin, Saco, and Connecticut rivers; it soon became a stopping point for hunters and travelers.

Proprietary rights to the Israel River Valley were originally granted in 1765 in seventy separate lots; Whipple capitalized on the failure of proprietors to settle the land, buying all of the rights to the township, called Dartmouth, in 1775. Having acquired all the property in Dartmouth, he proceeded to lease it out to tenant farmers and servants with the promise that, with success, they could eventually own the land.

Whipple used his considerable influence in New Hampshire politics to push for the construction of a road through the Western Notch. The road would be built, but not until after the War for Independence. The first road through the mountains was built in 1774, at the same time that Joseph Whipple was establishing his plantation at Dartmouth. The road pierced the Eastern Notch, next to the Great Mountain. The builder was Captain John Evans.

Among his Pequawket contemporaries, John Evans was most knowledgeable about road-building, not because of study,

rather necessity. He was not a surveyor or cartographer by pro-
fession, rather a hunter and farmer—the typical jack-of-all-
trades New Englander. Upon moving his family to Fryeburg,
and for the next decade afterward, Evans' major concern, like
that of all of his neighbors, was providing shelter, food, and
security for his family. He and others were often forced to
make the trip to Saco, Falmouth, Portsmouth, or Boston for
basic supplies. Luckily Evans owned the Mill Lot, where the
first grist mill was built by John Bucknell. No description survives of the mill, but it was probably a rustic horizontal mill,
where the force of the water pushed horizontal wooden blades,
spikes of a wooden or iron shaft connected to the mill stone.
Planting, harvesting, grinding grain to flour, hunting, fishing,
mending fences, caring for livestock, repairing carts, keeping
roads clear, and repairing primitive bridges that succumbed to
the force of a sudden freshet—such activities left little time
for entertainment or edification. Indeed the town was without
a meeting-house for many years and did not have a settled
minister until the Reverend William Fessenden took the job
in 1774. In the meantime the town relied on occasional ministers who visited to perform marriages and baptisms. Evans'
old employer, Timothy Walker, journeyed to Seven Lots for
said purposes in 1764 and returned again in October 1766, at
which time he baptized William, the Evans's sixth child. The
Reverend Timothy Walker, *Jr.* journeyed to "Pigwacket" in
1765. He visited many of his friends from Penacook and on
several occasions visited Evans at Lovewell's Pond, examining
the site of Lovewell's Battle, helping to unload "stores"
brought in "battow" (*bateaux*) from Saco, and hunting and
fishing. Harvard-educated Walker junior took time to write "a
deed for John Evans." Not surprisingly Walker "drank tea"
with others who appeared more cultivated—Colonel Joseph
Frye and Captain Henry Brown.

When Fryeburg was incorporated as a town in 1767, the
citizens elected Evans the *surveyor of highways*, which was
an office of the utmost importance for the isolated frontier
community. Town leaders constantly dreamed of and yearned

for roads to provide adequate communications and routes to convey trade goods. As surveyor of highways, it was Evans' job "to prevent or remove obstructions; to keep roads and bridges in repair." But the moist climate and hilly landscape rarely cooperated. Washed out roads and fallen or nonexistent bridges enhanced Fryeburg's unending sense of living on the edge of civilization. Yet there was great potential in Fryeburg's location, which lay on the logical line of travel from the Cohos Intervales to the Saco and beyond to the seacoast. Conway, a new community just west of Fryeburg upstream on the Saco at the junction of the Ellis River, also sensed the economic potential inherent in its location. Conway residents such as John Evans' old comrade Andrew McMillan pushed the provincial government to pay for the building of a road through one or both of the notches of the White Mountains that separated the new communities of Shelburne, Dartmouth, Northumberland, and Lancaster from Conway and Fryeburg. Such a road would unite the Saco, Androscoggin, Ammonoosuc, Israel, and Connecticut river valleys, which otherwise were irrevocably separated by the mountains.

In 1774 the Province of New Hampshire hired John Evans to direct the building of a road to link Conway with Shelburne. Evans managed a road crew of axe-men and drivers, some of whom, like himself, knew enough about the compass to perform ad hoc surveying. The landscape was singularly unenviable. The thirty miles that separated Conway on the Saco from Shelburne on the Androscoggin comprised a continual ascent of heavily forested land, where outcrops of massive granite boulders competed with miry bogs of stagnant water and thick, moss-covered soil. Few meadows interspersed the ubiquitous fir-tree forests of hemlock, pitch pine, and the indomitable white pine. Rays of sunlight scarcely penetrated the green canopy. Winds high above rocked the immense trunks back and forth, producing eerie creaks and groans to break the otherwise interminable silence. Biting black flies and stinging mosquitoes held sway. Rodents popped their heads from hidden dens and scurried off, but larger game rarely appeared. Rattlesnakes abounded and were quickly dispatched with blows of the axe.

Evans and his men tread on a forest floor that was a pine-needle carpet, soft and peaceful. Tall ferns and raspberry thickets provided beauty, food, and slow travel. Nature, fortunately, gave the road-builders a handy guide. The Ellis River was wonderfully hazardous, stone-filled, infrequently deep, filled with incredibly clear, extremely cold, rapidly moving water. The Indians long ago paralleled the river on long hunts, and their paths still remained. As unchanging, yet never quite the same, was the Ellis: natural dams of huge boulders and contorted tree branches, intermittent water falls, the recurrent confluence of river with rushing brooks, deep sapphire pools alternating with shallows, a collage of colors and shapes—such was the pattern of change and the movement of aeons.

The Ellis flowed north to south between massive peaks, carving a narrow valley that represented the most efficient route for travel. The Ellis was, however, hardly a river to accommodate a canoe, and the forest grew close to the shore, forcing the construction of a road for ease of movement and proper conveyance of goods. Road-building had become something of a science by 1774, involving knowledge of geometry and trigonometry, the use of sophisticated instruments such as the theodolite, and the application of crushed stones, well-graded, to form the road base. The Shelburne Road, the construction of which John Evans led in 1774, had the benefit of none of these materials, tools, and knowledge. The Shelburne Road was a frontier road, a pass amid the wilderness, befitting its builder. The knowledge Evans used was an intuitive sense of direction, of lines of ascent and descent, of what appeared to be soil that would be sufficiently hard and stony to withstand the sudden freshet. His tools were an iron-headed axe fitted to an ash handle, an adze of the same construction, and a compass to gauge direction. Whether or not Evans knew of the angle of declension and "the variation of the [compass] needle" from true north to magnetic north is doubtful. Perhaps the road team included a professional surveyor who made allowance for the natural variance of the compass. Perhaps, too, the team carried a Gunter's Chain, the most efficient means of measuring distance, although even at this time some surveyors relied on a simple notched rope for measurement. The road bed consisted of packed earth, the quality and smoothness of which depended on the quality of the axe work in reducing stumps to ground level. Low elevations, bog and marsh land, if unavoidable, were fitted with primitive pine causeways. The men avoided having to cross streams at all costs unless beavers had already done the work—then the dam was tested to see whether or not it could bear the weight of horse and rider, or team and cart. The surveying team went first, measuring, estimating, and guessing, notching trees to indicate the path. They sought pitch-pine land, which was typically dry and sandy, relatively smooth, and often had fewer trees though much underbrush. The axe-men followed the surveyors, cursing the ferns and thickets, yearning for substantial tall pines upon which to display their skill, hoping to leave in their wake plentiful loads for the teamsters to drag away. Unavoidable stumps were dug up and dragged out and away as were large stones.

Evans knew that the untold labor put into building the Shelburne Road could easily come to naught should the anticipated travel, the wagonloads of trade goods, and the new settlers seeking new land not materialize. Belknap learned from Evans that "when a road is constantly used, the feet of horses and cattle keep down the growth of bushes, which sprout, with great luxuriance, from the roots of felled trees; but if the road be neglected, these young shoots render travelling extremely inconvenient; and it is more difficult to clear them a second time." For the Shelburne Road to remain a road and not turn into a hidden path in the wilderness, new towns would have to be built along the route to shoulder the burden of upkeep; local surveyors of highways would have to take over to prevent the labor of Evans and his men from becoming useless and forgotten. But time would not be kind to Shelburne Road.

One spring day in June 1774, after weeks of road building,

having reached the highlands above which the Great Mountain towers, a sprightly group of axe-men obtained permission to ascend the mountain in search of the precious stones so long sought by explorers but never discovered. They ascended the mountain from the southeast, probably up the ridge known today as Boott Spur; they found along the way, "in one of the deep gullies" on the south side of the mountain, "a body of snow thirteen feet deep, and so hard, as to bear them." They did not find precious stones. Two weeks later, the road builders having reached the watershed that separates the southward flowing Ellis River from the northward flowing Peabody River—a height of land once a beaver pond, now a beautiful meadow—John Evans decided to follow in the wake of the other men and ascend the Great Mountain. He journeyed again from the east, paralleling a descending mountain river up a rocky ridge between massive ravines, north and south. Near Boott Spur, south of the summit, he found in the same spot as the others snow that was five feet deep—on June 19! Evans then proceeded north to the Sugar Loaf, the highest summit, which he ascended. Not the type to leave a written record of his accomplishment nor even to pound into stone his initials, Evans still yearned to leave behind—for who's benefit he was uncertain—a reminder, a monument, to recall the moment upon the peak. So he put his hat under a stone, and quickly descended to the much warmer region of the work camp.

Four months later another man of quite a different background ascended the Great Mountain. Very little survives to document the life of Nicholas Austin of Wolfeborough. He was a personal friend of Governor Wentworth and owned land near the governor's plantation at Lake Winnipesaukee. Austin was also a loyalist who must have changed his political sympathies during the Revolution. In John Wentworth's letter to Jeremy Belknap of November 18, 1774, he refers to Austin as "the man whom some modern patriots at Rochester tyrannically insulted and abused for the sake of Liberty." Rochester patriots accused Austin of recruiting craftsmen to journey to Massachusetts to build barracks for redcoats. Austin survived the war and was still living in the Lake Winnipesaukee region in 1785, at a time when former loyalists were still very much unwelcome. In 1774 Nicholas Austin was a mountain climber.

Wentworth wrote Belknap in November 1774 for two reasons: to "return your MSS. chapter," the first, "of the History of New Hampshire," which described the supposed journey of Captain Walter Neal to the White Mountains. Second, Wentworth wanted to correct Belknap's assumption that Neal ascended the highest mountain, Great Mountain, by including a long description of Nicholas Austin's journey to the White Mountains in October. Wentworth heard from Austin that "he ascended the second in height and magnitude, which he describes exactly as Captain Neal did. But discovering a large mountain E.N.E. from this he travelled about eight miles to the bottom. Ascending to the top or apex, he found it far exceeded all others in the horizon, computing it to be two miles higher than the adjacent country." Since Captain Neal did not leave behind a record of his journey, as far as we know, Wentworth was referring to Belknap's account in the *History of New-Hampshire* of Neal journeying with Henry Josselyn and Darby Field, which included a reference to a pond on the summit of the Great Mountain. Austin's mountain, "second in height," *did* have a pond on the summit. Wentworth therefore concluded, "I am inclined to think Captain Neal was mistaken in supposing he had explored the highest mountain. Besides the unsuspected credibility of Mr. Austin, my own observations in the year 1772, when my curiosity led me on to the second, which I suppose Neal's mountain, perfectly agree with his relation."

Intrigued and perplexed, Belknap investigated further, finding the chance, nineteen months later, to himself interview Nicholas Austin. Belknap recorded the interview in "Several Accounts of the White Mountains":

Nicholas Austin's Account of the White Hills taken from His Own Mouth, June 24, 1776.
The first week in October 1774. He with 8 others visited these

Mountains on a report of their containing silver and precious stones—which report by the way is altogether false.—

They encamped and lodged at the foot of the highest Mountain on the south side, near a brook which descended, waiting several days for fair weather. While they tarried below they frequently observed the Mountain to be obscured and even totally hid by the clouds. At length on a clear morning they began their ascent at the rising of the sun (which is ¼ after 6 H°). They went through a thick growth of fir and spruce shrubs the tops of which not being much more than a man's height were knotted together so that it was difficult getting through. The height of these shrubs diminished as they rose the hill. When they had left them they came to whortleberry bushes about 4 or 5 inches high which had both ripe and green berries. They also saw a species of berries which they had never before seen. When they had got through these they came to a space covered with moss and not very steep, the moss about 2 or 3 inches deep and a rock underneath. Here they walked at a great pace and could have galloped horses if they had had any. In this space, he observed several small ponds of water and some spots full of very smooth stones which he supposed may be wet at some seasons. This mossy space continues to the foot of the Sugar Loaf which consists entirely of grey rock without either earth or moss and is judged a mile in height. They clambered up the rocks which are fixt and uneven so as to serve as steps and in an hour and half from the foot of the Sugar Loaf they reached the highest top of the Mountain, a few minutes after 12 a clock. Here they sat down and rested being much fatigued, but found no difficulty in breathing. The top is a rough rock and may contain half an acre as he judges but there was no water as some travellers have reported nor any hollow capable of containing any quantity.

There are 4 Mountains properly called the White Mountains. They appear to belong to one ridge which he judges may be 20 miles in length lying NE and SW. He could discover the Atlantic Ocean very plain and many ponds and lakes and rivers of which he did not know the names of all. He could see the high land between Connecticut and St. Lawrence River. From the easterly side about ⅔ds up issued 3 small streams which pursued different courses down the Mountain. In the fissures of the rock he found a root resembling a parsnip and brought away some of the seed but being informed it was a species of the hyoscyamus and therefore dangerous he has thrown it away. He observed no animals but hares which were among the shrubs and a species of fowl which he has since been informed is a heath-hen. Of these they shot several which were fine meat. They descended and arrived at their former lodging about sunset, being all very stout men and used to the woods: having tarried an hour on the top of the Mountain. They found an old hat covered with a stone on the top of the Mountain, and they left one of their knapsacks under the same stone.

Belknap was never entirely convinced that Captain Neal's mountain was not the same as Nicholas Austin's mountain. In the ten years between Governor Wentworth's 1774 letter and his own journey to the White Mountains in 1784, Belknap discovered the two accounts (which he transcribed in "Several Accounts of the White Mountains") describing Neal, Josselyn, and Field wading knee deep in a pond on or near the summit of the Great Mountain, as well as Captain Wells' account of finding a frozen pond on the summit in 1725. These compared nicely with John Josselyn's description in *New-Englands Rarities Discovered*. But how to explain the absence of a pond in 1774?

Mountain peaks are rarely disturbed, and then usually by men of peace. Human conflicts do not penetrate the haunting silence of the foggy summit, nor do they halt the brisk wind of a sunny day soaring over the bald and stony top. In the valley below bloodshed might occur, but it stands in contradiction to the universal sameness, the timeless natural order of things, symbolized by the lonely and distant mountain.

No one wanted war—and yet it came. For the inhabitants of the seacoast of northern New England the War for Independence meant the glorious struggle for freedom but the halt of trade and economic deprivation as well. The closing of Boston's harbor and the destruction of Falmouth, Maine, terrorized and impoverished clergymen such as Daniel Little of Kennebunk and Jeremy Belknap of Dover. Both men joined the cause, if reluctantly—Belknap felt himself an Englishman and respected loyalists such as Governor John Wentworth. But reason and the will of God seemed to point to American independence. Belknap supported the American cause with his pen and in the pulpit. Daniel Little attempted unsuccessfully to devise a new way to produce steel, hence to contribute to the arming of patriots. Other men of New Hampshire and Maine joined the ranks of fighters. At Rochester, on the upper Cocheco, farmers such as George Place and Enoch Wingate joined the local militia. Ensign Place was stationed at Portsmouth and Boston, while Wingate served three years and was at Fort Ticonderoga in 1777. Settlers of the upper Connecticut, Israel, Ammonoosuc, Androscoggin, and Saco rivers feared a revisitation of Indian raids, as in years before, this time instigated by the British rather than the French. Indeed the silence of the northern forest gave way to shouts and cries of conflict. Indian raiders followed old trails from Canada to attack the frontier towns of Bethel, Maine, and Shelburne, New Hampshire. They looted, kidnapped, and killed, driving the hapless settlers into hiding or makeshift forts; some fled south to Conway for protection. At the end of July the first band of raiders, seeking to attack the towns of the Upper Cohos, journeyed west along old trails north of the White Mountains. In their path was Joseph Whipple's plantation at Dartmouth.

Tradition has it that Whipple saw the invaders as they approached his house, but being without help save for his housekeeper, Mrs. Hight, he could attempt but a futile defense. He decided against rashness and chose to await, patiently, an alternative form of rescue. Acting as if he suspected nothing, Whipple treated the natives as guests, to which they responded by taking him prisoner, declaring their intention to take him north to Canada to await a ransom for their prize. Whipple slyly asked for time to change into traveling clothes, to which the natives agreed. Mrs. Hight, sensing Whipple's ruse, instinctively played along. Wife to James Hight, a struggling tenant farmer, Mrs. Hight was made of sturdy stuff; she refused to allow fear to interfere with what she imagined to be Whipple's silent request. She brought the invaders food and drink and otherwise distracted them so that Whipple easily escaped from a bedroom window. He hustled to the distant fields, where the men worked as yet unalarmed—and unarmed. Having fooled the natives once, Whipple was determined to repeat the attempt. Ordering the men to shoulder thick boards and sticks as if armed, he marched them in good formation, as to war.

The natives, by now in search of the escapee, spied the distant army and waiting for neither further information nor battle fled headlong into the woods, gone for the time being.

On the first of August several more parties of raiders returned to the Androscoggin Valley, attacking Bethel and Shelburne. Men such as Colonel Whipple busied themselves at Conway, trying to raise troops for the defense. Fryeburg immediately responded, sending twenty-three militiamen north. Captain Henry Brown, writing from Brownfield, a town adjacent to Fryeburg, on August 7, 1781, requested that the State of Massachusetts send reinforcements: "I know of no man more Sutable for the business than Lt John Evans of Fryeburg[;] his knowledge of the Country and Experience in the Service Renders him very capible for it." Evans, a member of Fryeburg's Committee of Safety, was duly commissioned; he led troops north to Bethel, but by then the enemy had retreated.

Jeremy Belknap, meanwhile, looking beyond the war to grander phenomena and sublime moments, ascended the small hill called Agamenticus, across the Piscataqua River at York, Maine. From its modest summit Belknap could see

a most enchanting prospect. The cultivated parts of the country, especially on the south and southwest, appear as a beautiful garden, intersected by the majestick river Piscataqua, its bays and branches. The immense ranges of mountains on the north and northwest afford a sublime spectacle; and on the sea-side the various indentings of the coast from Cape Ann to Cape Elizabeth are plainly in view in clear day; and the wide Atlantick stretches to the east as far as the power of vision extends.

Agamenticus afforded a vision of the past and the future. Belknap could see what lured explorers such as John Smith to discover and claim the Isles of Shoals and Martin Pring to voyage up the churning waters of the Piscataqua River. He could see why seamen and merchants chose the deep harbors of Strawbery Banke, which grew to become the shipbuilding and trading center of Portsmouth. He could see what attracted fishermen, lumbermen, and missionaries to the estuaries of the Great Bay, to the small rivers of the Squamscott, Lamprey, and Cocheco. He could see as well the distant, seemingly impenetrable White Mountains. From Agamenticus Belknap could see the wilderness poles of the forest and the sea, with New England towns uncomfortably nestled in between. His gaze moved from sea to land, from the never-ending fathoms of the blue-green ocean to the endless abyss of the vast white hills. To conquer both is to know, to gain extended awareness, to become enlightened. But to know is to penetrate, to journey thither, to conquer the monsters of the imagination, the legends of the deep.

The vision from Mount Agamenticus placed in Belknap's mind the desire to ascend ever greater peaks, to look down from ever higher summits. From the summit of the small hill he imagined the summit of the Great Mountain. There stands a great gulf between dream and reality. But from Belknap's experience would come, in 1784, the attempt to ascend the pinnacle that dominates New England: the Great Mountain.

Belknap frequently wrote of his dreams and aspirations to his best friend Ebenezer Hazard of Philadelphia. The two men shared an interest in the study of natural and human history and wrote long letters back and forth sharing their investigations into the worlds of historical documents and the natural environment. Hazard, the Surveyor of Post Roads of the United States during the war, was always traveling, checking post roads and establishing communication posts. He often journeyed north of Boston and could occasionally see the distant White Mountains, which yielded a design to one day visit them. Belknap, knowing his friend's mutual interest, would sometimes send Hazard communications about the mountains. During the summer of 1781 Belknap was able to persuade his acquaintance, General John Sullivan of Durham, New Hampshire, to part with a copy of a letter he had recently written to the secretary of the French ambassador to the United States, Monsieur Marbois. The letter so fascinated Belknap that he transcribed it in "Several Accounts of the White Mountains":

*Account of the White Mountain in a Letter from General Sullivan
to Monsieur Marbois — December, 1780.*

The White Mountains are perhaps the most remarkable in the world.
They appear like a white cloud and though at the distance of 100
miles from the sea coast, may in clear weather be discovered at a
much greater distance at sea, than the highest lands on the sea shore.
Their white appearance is owing to bright rocks and a white moss
which seems to cover the whole. There are 3 of those hills ranging
nearly N.E. to S.W. which is the general course of mountains in
America. The E. and W. of those mountains have with difficulty been
ascended, that in the center never has though often attempted. It is
called the Sugar-Loaf from the resemblance it bears to it when viewed
at a distance. Many persons have marched for several days to gain
the summit but found it impossible. The weather in the midst of
summer becomes intolerably cold, and the trees gradually diminish
in size as you ascend, till they are reduced to meer shrubs and by
farther continuance you find neither tree, shrub nor plant; a white
moss is the only product of the severity of its peculiar climate will
permit. By this time, the weary traveller finding himself in the midst
of winter, without fewel, the difficulty of ascending increased by the
almost perpendicular declivity of the hill, without even a shrub to
support him in advancing or to prevent his tumbling headlong from
some of the dangerous precipices, finds himself under a necessity of
giving over the dangerous adventure. The savages sensible of the difficulty never attempt to ascend it, and endeavor to dissuade others
from it. From the tops of these mountains run a variety of streams
some forming delightful cascades and others the most astonishing
cataracts. In some places you will see a large stream gushing from
the Mountain, falling down the rocks perpendicularly more than 500
feet. These streams form lakes in the country below from which issue
a variety of rivers.

Such a description, which both Belknap and Hazard knew
was filled with errors, and which excited their laughter, nevertheless only fueled Hazard's desire to journey thither. He
planned on going in August, but reports of the enemy incursions into the region and the attempted kidnapping of Joseph
Whipple made him think again; he wrote Belknap in September that "the tour (at least *mine*) to the White Hills is post-
poned. The mere gratification of curiosity is not a sufficient
inducement to me to run the risk of either my life or my liberty." Six months later Belknap wrote Hazard that "I do hope
to see them myself this fall, if there is no further irruption of
the enemy in that quarter, and I shall most sincerely wish for

the company of my friend Hazard." But other matters intervened, so that Belknap contented himself in September 1782
with a more modest journey following the Salmon Falls River
upstream to its head near Moose Mountain, which he ascended. "But the growth was so tall and thick on the top that
my fatigue in climbing was not repaid by any pleasure in the
prospect as I expected. There was a pond on the top of the
mountain of about a quarter of an acre with water. In another
place near it I found a swampy cavity with flags and rushes,
but the water was dried. The ascent and descent of this mountain cost me four hour's hard labour, and you may guess I slept
that night without waking."

Meanwhile Belknap heard of other attempts to ascend the
Great Mountain. During the dreary days of war many dreamed
of the shining gems, the hidden treasure, undiscovered in
mountain caves, cliffs, and flumes. News of peace in the spring
of 1783 brought with it a joyful release from the distractions
of war. Once again when mountain people saw glimmering
lights on the Great Mountain they thought not of spies sending coded messages but of carbuncles gleaming under the glare
of moonlight and stars; when they heard the thundering
booms echoing in the mountains on a clear day they thought
not of enemy cannon but of Passaconaway's curse. Peace com-
pelled Nehemiah Porter, who resided in Massachusetts but
who owned land in the town of Shelburne, and his friend Ingalls (either of two brothers, Benjamin or Daniel), a Shelburne
farmer, to try their luck ascending the Great Mountain in September 1783. Ingalls had journeyed to the mountain on several
previous occasions—exactly when is unclear. On one of his
previous attempted ascents he brought back lead with a few
veins of silver showing through. Now, with Porter's help, he
sought the mother lode.

Belknap heard about their failed attempt from the Reverend
Joseph Haven of Rochester, who got the story from the Reverend William Fessenden, pastor of Fryeburg. Any news of ascents of the Great Mountain, especially when they involved
the search for precious stones, traveled quickly about the

towns of the upper Saco and upper Androscoggin. That Fessenden knew about the ascent indicates that John Evans would have known as well. Belknap and Haven were old friends who shared an interest in the natural and human history of the White Mountains. Haven could see the Great Mountain from the parsonage; he frequently recorded his observations of the appearance and probable weather of the mountains during the four seasons. Haven's account of the journey of Porter and Ingalls reads:

*Account of the White Mountain as Told by Mr. Fesenden to Mr. Haven.*

Mr. Nehemiah Porter of Andover in company with Mr. Ingalls of Shelburne ascended them the first week in September 1783, in search of ore of which Ingalls had some time before taken some and found it to consist mostly of lead but with some mixture of silver. He said it was near Shelburne Road and supposed he could soon find it but was disappointed. They took the New River so called and followed the stream upward till they found it parted into three branches; they took the middle one which was much less than the Eastern-most. Upon this middle stream they found large rocks, some of which appeared of the bigness of a common hay-stack rolled some way from their former bed. Large trees torn up by the roots and tumbled down the mountain with old logs and other rubbish. They pursued this stream till they found it issue out of the Mountain. They ascended till they came to ice and snow of some inches depth (NB the ice was made and the snow had fallen *this* season). The cold was so intense that though their exercise in climbing was hard and they had on outside garments yet they wanted another. The middle stream is large enough for a mill-stream and the falls stupendous, some of them seemed no less than 100 feet.

During succeeding months Belknap became convinced that the time was right for his own journey to the White Mountains. Belknap was anything but an adventurer, rather a scholar. He was obese and had not enjoyed good health for many years. But his drive and his imagination made up for his physical infirmities and limitations. He had tramped throughout the Piscataqua region, visited the Merrimack and Connecticut rivers, and journeyed into the foothills of the White Mountains numerous times. His ministerial duties were many, as were his children (six); his income was slight and recently nonexistent; his wife suffered from a chronic nervous complaint and feared her husband's extensive absence. Even so Belknap was presently at work on the second volume of his *History of New-Hampshire*, having just sent the first volume to press at the end of 1783. A careful scholar and researcher, he needed firsthand information if he were to pen an accurate natural history of the state. "I do not chuse to be a Second-hand author any more than need requires," he wrote a friend; "I should chuse to visit and be personally acquainted with every part of the Country I mean to describe." Belknap liked to think of himself as a predator after knowledge of the natural and human past. This "wolfish behavior" convinced him to reject all the varied reasons he and others had for him *not* to go. He would go, but when?

Time hides from us how John Evans, by this time a captain in the militia, was contacted to be the guide, or pilot, of an expedition to the White Mountains. Perhaps Belknap met Reverend Fessenden of Fryeburg through Reverend Haven and heard from Fessenden of Evans' experience and knowledge. Perhaps Daniel Little of Kennebunk had traveled up the Saco, or knew someone (such as the Reverend Paul Coffin of Buxton, Maine) who had, and had heard of Evans as the likely choice to guide men of science. Another possibility is that Joseph Whipple knew Evans from their mutual experiences defending the Androscoggin Valley from Indian raiders during the war, and he made the arrangement. With clear documents lacking, one must speculate that Belknap was the mastermind behind the plan to organize several scientists, including Colonel Whipple and Reverend Little, to be led by the backwoodsman John Evans to the Great Mountain. Belknap wrote several of his friends of his intentions. He informed Little to prepare for June or July, to which Little responded that by chance he had simultaneously received a letter from the Reverend Manasseh Cutler of Ipswich (Hamilton), Massachusetts, who intended on journeying with a company of Massachusetts scientists and adventurers in July. Little took the liberty of inviting Cutler, whose "principle object is botany," to go botanizing with Bel-

knap, Little, and Whipple. Cutler agreed. Belknap also wrote
of the planned journey, on Independence Day 1784, to Ebenezer Hazard of Philadelphia: "I expect, next week, to set out
on a land tour to the White Mountains, in company with several gentlemen of a scientific turn. . . . If I live to come back,
you may depend on such a description as I may be able to give.
I shall wish you one of the party." Hazard, a new father, unable
to go, responded: "O that I could have gone with you! It was
once my expectation. But I have no right to expect to visit
*every* place in the world, and I can fully rely upon the testi-
mony of your senses. Should you not have been disappointed,
I dare say I shall have a very accurate description of those
famous hills; and, probably, such an account of them as may
make a suitable memoir to be laid before the [American Phil-
osophical] Society," of which both Belknap and Hazard were
members.

Belknap's commitment to the journey dramatically increased when, in June, he heard a secondhand account of a
purported scientific expedition to the Great Mountain, led "by
a certain German who pretends to be a great mineralogist"—
an apparent pseudo-scientist who otherwise remains unidentified. They "went to these Mountains, and pretended that
they had discovered something of great value, which they
made a profound secret of"—which naturally made a scientist
such as Belknap, who believed in the free and open communication of scientific discoveries, very suspicious. But this had
always been the way of the mountains, a place of undisguised
danger and hidden mystery, a place that could not but be the
focus of legend and the unbelievable. Belknap knew more
about the natural history of the White Mountains, and the
human story to penetrate and come to know them, than any
of his contemporaries. He was a rationalist who was tired of
speculation and fairy tales. The time had come for the mysteries of the mountains to meet their match in the objectivity
and incredulity of America's "sons of science."

*Chapter Four*

# THE FRONTIER OF SCIENCE

Just after noon on Tuesday, July 20, 1784, friends, acquaintances, scientists, clergymen, students, and adventurers—numbering six in all—rendezvoused at the parsonage of Jeremy Belknap, minister of the First Parish of Dover, New Hampshire. Daniel Little, minister of the First Parish of Kennebunk, Maine, was already a frequent visitor to New Hampshire, through which one must pass to reach Massachusetts. Little had also spent a rich and memorable childhood living on the New Hampshire frontier just north of Haverhill, Massachusetts. As a young man he had preached at nearby Brentwood, New Hampshire, and at Portsmouth, before he settled in Maine. Little could have taken one of several roads to Dover after he set out on horseback from Kennebunk during the third week of July. Perhaps he took the path paralleling the northern shore of the Piscataqua, crossing by ferry the Salmon Falls River, then riding the remaining few miles paralleling the Cocheco River to the falls, where Belknap lived. But let us imagine that Little, who frequently journeyed to Portsmouth on business, took the less direct yet more well-traveled route from Kennebunk to York, in the shadow of Mount Agamenticus, then on to Kittery, a bustling seaport on the northern shore of the Piscataqua. Little then took the ferry boat—perhaps resembling the single-sailed gundalow, so often seen in these waters—across the Piscataqua to Strawbery Banke, the center of Portsmouth's commercial activity. The distance from Kittery to Strawbery Banke is less than a mile of churning, unpredictable water, and even that is broken by Badger's Island. Portsmouth at this time had four to five thousand people. The town was nearly one hundred and fifty years old, having been the object of settlement and growth ever since the English explorer Martin Pring had spied the deep, secure harbors. One imagines the ferry docking at Puddle Dock, where more goods than passengers were unloaded, from which Little proceeded down narrow paths lined with cheery saltbox homes, taverns, merchant's mansions, and shops, until he reached Market Square. The red-bricked First Parish Church, its white spire piercing the sky, still dominates Market Square. Little and Belknap's mutual friend the Reverend Joseph Buckminster, recently married and a new father, ruled the First Parish. Doubtless Little spent the night at Portsmouth, for what better place was there than the Buckminster home, graced with the presence of Mrs. Buckminster, the former Miss Stevens, a well-known beauty? The next morning Little proceeded down North Street for the long ride to Newington and Bloody Point, where the ferry crossed the Piscataqua to Dover Point. The Point juts out into the watery confluence of a host of rivers that forms the Great Bay and Piscataqua River. The point is on rising ground; some gentlemen thought it was a grand site for a city, but it was then uninhabited. From here it was a brief journey by horseback along the dirt road, past the busy tavern, noisy sawmills, and clapboard meeting-house to the Belknap homestead.

Meanwhile Manasseh Cutler and John Heard of Ipswich, Dr. Joshua Fisher of Beverly, and two Harvard students, Dudley Hubbard and John Bartlett, who were on quite an extensive field trip, journeyed north by stage, their horses trailing behind. The day was overcast, with intermittent rain. At Newburyport, a small town on the Massachusetts north shore with a deep harbor dotted with sails, they ferried across the wide Merrimack to New Hampshire. From there they took the same path as today's Route One to Hampton Falls. They spent the night at Captain Wells' Tavern, where, perchance, they heard marvelous stories of the White Mountains. The next morning they rose early and journeyed northwest through the peaceful town of Kensington to Exeter, a town built on shipbuilding, lumbering, and trade, situated at the mouth of the Squamscot on the southwestern side of the Great Bay. Here they break-fasted before paralleling the north shore of the Squamscot to Stratham, from which they rode on horseback to Newmarket on the Lamprey River. Towns like Newmarket that hugged the Great Bay owed their existence to the forest and the sea. It was rare to find such a town at peace from the grinding hum of the sawmill. From Newmarket the path was an easy one to Durham on the Oyster River, Darby Field's onetime home, and then to Dover.

The Reverend and Mrs. Jeremy Belknap welcomed their visitors from Maine and Massachusetts to their comfortable two-story home. Ruth Belknap was the product of genteel Boston society. Descended from the Byles and Mather families, well-educated but extremely sensitive, delicate, Ruth had survived the Dover frontier the best she could, enduring cheerfully if not very successfully the anxieties and privation of wartime as well as her husband's frustration at being an insignificant clergyman. She was formal and elegant, if her surroundings were not, and she set a nice table, at which the gentlemen sat for dinner before beginning the journey. Belknap and Cutler met for the first time. The two were like-minded in their focus on practical theology and their interest in natural science. Otherwise they could not have been more different.

Manasseh Cutler was born in 1742 to a Connecticut farm family who prospered enough to send their son to Yale, from which he graduated in 1765. After a brief stint studying law and teaching grammar school, he turned to the study of "divinity," as he wrote in his journal, and was ordained in 1771. He settled in a small Massachusetts town near the seashore and practiced his vocation in a solid, worthwhile manner. Speculative theology bored Cutler, who focused on Christian morality and commonsense religion; this left time for other, scientific pursuits, of which he was particularly fond. Cutler's personal motto, taken from Virgil, was: "Happy is the man who is able to know the course of things." He applied this motto to all of his intellectual queries. Cutler was a quantitative, precise man who knew there was an order to things, a

*Sketch of Manasseh Cutler.* Manasseh Cutler was the principal scientist of the Belknap/Cutler expedition of 1784. He returned to Mount Washington twenty years later, in 1804. *New Hampshire Historical Society.*

carefully planned structure according to all that was lawful and reasonable. Humans, having the capacity to reason and to recognize the reasonable, could therefore come to know this order by observation, experimentation, the recording and analysis of data, and the communication of results to others. Cutler was a scientist. Fascinated by scientific instruments, he used the microscope to see what lies hidden inside and the telescope to peer into the otherwise hidden realm of space. At night he scanned the heavens for the aurora borealis and for noteworthy constellations. On less humble occasions he tracked the transit of Mercury across the sun or analyzed a lunar eclipse. He was one of many American astronomers who tracked the course of Venus across the disk of the sun in June 1769. Many nights he studied and drew in his journal the shape and movements of Jupiter and its moons. Like all amateur astronomers, he was simultaneously mystified and fascinated by comets. Not a metaphysician, he was content to record observations rather than to propose solutions for the existence of celestial phenomena.

By the time the war broke out in 1775, Cutler had practiced law and medicine, had been a merchant at Martha's Vineyard, and had cured the sick of physical as well as spiritual illnesses. He served as a chaplain during the Revolution and continued his experiments and observations. In 1779 we find him repeating many of Franklin's experiments in electricity. In 1780 he declared: "The only solid foundation for advances in the real knowledge of nature, whose wonderful and secret operations are so involved and intricate, so far out of the reach of our sense, must be made by a regular series of experiments." An ad hoc meteorologist, he kept track of weather conditions, changes in temperature, and the overall impact of climatic change on vegetation. After much effort he was able to obtain a barometer to facilitate the keeping of what he called his "Meteorological Journal."

During the war he became a practicing physician, chiefly out of his love for botany. He learned to inoculate patients against the smallpox. After 1780 Cutler's inquiries focused

particularly upon plant life. Fascinated by the efforts of the
Swedish scientist Carolus Linneaus to classify and catalogue
plants and animals, Cutler incorporated the system into his
own study of American flora and fauna. Such were Cutler's
reasons for journeying to the White Mountains: to collect,
catalogue, and study the various ferns, grasses, mosses, flow-
ers, and trees of the mountains. How do valley and mountain
growth compare? How does the height and temperature of the
mountains affect vegetation? And what of the soil, the rain,
and the winds of the mountains?

So many were the questions. So few were the answers. Yet
upon such answers depended the future of the United States.
Agriculture was the basis of the country, and botany the basis
of agriculture. The botanist Cutler expressed his patriotism
through science. The nascent American republic depended
upon improvement, growth, progress. The future lay in the
untapped resources, the undiscovered knowledge, the unexplored lands of the north and west. The White Mountains were
just the beginning.

What direction his life would take down the unexplored
paths of America was unknown to Cutler in 1784. Yet his
character was a signpost for the future. The journey stripped
him of his clerical robes, took him from the stale air of the
pulpit, opened his heart and mind to new challenges and experiences. Revealed was a determined, dogmatic man. Well-
set, strong, and athletic, with a firm New England jaw, a broad
forehead, and a steady gaze, he sat a horse well and fit the part
of an adventurer. The hired men on the journey would discover in Cutler the resolution and haughtiness of command
rather than the benevolence and humility of the divine. To his
equals he was polite, distant, a silent disputer, a charming if
hidden man.

Very little, by choice and by nature, was hidden in the life
and character of Jeremy Belknap. He was candid, honest at
times to the point of giving offense, yet good-natured and well-
meaning with a disarming wit. In his amateur way Belknap
was a sporadic experimentalist, more an observer and recorder

of natural phenomena. He countered Cutler's reason and objectivity with a touch of the intuitive and romantic. Precision and quantification had their place, but only next to wonder, faith, even piety. Whereas Cutler came to the study of nature through curiosity and the proclivity toward erudition, Belknap approached nature with utter humility. To Belknap, nature— natural and human experience—is "elder Scripture, writ by God's own hand," best studied and understood by the scientist filled with religious awe and love for the benevolent creator.

Writing, of all the forms of personal expression, obsessed Jeremy Belknap. He was at the same time a poet, novelist, epistler, essayist, and historian. Belknap approached all of his literary endeavors as if he were involved in a personal discourse with the humans of a past time. He engaged in a constant dialogue with the past—his was a true antiquarian perspective. His life was an ongoing search into the literary, physical, emotional, and spiritual documents of the past, hence his interest in White Mountain history, which he understood to be the tale of human interaction with the natural environment.

The road out of Dover awaited the travelers. The coolness of the morning vanished before the July heat of midday when Belknap, Cutler, Little and the rest sat down to dinner to gain strength for the journey. Ruth Belknap served them a traveler's meal of pork and greens, perhaps, or fish with potatoes from the Belknap's garden. After dinner the men checked their gear and saddlebags. It was hot and dusty when they waved their farewells to Mrs. Belknap and set off upon the road to Rochester. The breeze blew in from the east as they traveled northwest paralleling the descending Cocheco upriver. Along the way they could see the town of "Summersworth" in the distance, east of the river. They spent the night at the home of Joseph Haven, who had resided at Rochester eight years. Scarcely any evidence of Joseph Haven's Rochester remains today; the sleepy rural village of 1784 became a bustling factory town within a century. Nevertheless in places the landscape still appears from behind the streets and buildings, revealing distant hills, blue on the horizon, and farther on the White Mountains. The Great Mountain could be spied from Haven's parsonage. Cutler recorded in his journal that "at this house we have a very extensive prospect in every direction; we calculate" the distance to the mountains "at 90 miles." Haven often spent his mornings observing the changing colors and the drama of competing weather systems waging war atop the summit of the Great Mountain. Unable or unwilling to accompany the others, Haven retired to his armchair to record his observations upon their departure. He would continue to explore the mountains in his own way, with his eyes, his telescope, and his imagination.

Haven recommended as an initial guide for the journey George Place, a veteran of the war who knew well the dangers of the frontier and was experienced with the ways of the axe and the compass. Place earned four dollars guiding men into an unknown that, until recently, was forbidding and hazardous. Also joining the expedition, apparently for adventure's sake, was Enoch Wingate, whose credentials included his wartime experiences. Led by these veterans of war and wilderness, the men "traveled fifteen miles in Rochester" upon "plain, pine land, thin soil, houses low and poor." They "made a stage at Joseph Plummer's," in which they paralleled the Salmon Falls River and passed by three small hills that reminded Cutler of cobblestones as well as a much larger hill called Moose Mountain. Cutler noted in his journal that Moose Mountain "is very wooded, mostly oak, and in form nearly oval. The country to the north very mountainous, and its appearance has a most noble effect." The view whetted their appetites for climbing. When they arrived at Wakefield and passed through "fine fields of rye, peas, and Indian corn planted on new ground," they developed commensurate appetites for dinner that were satisfied at Captain David Copp's tavern. Copp proudly told them that the soil of Wakefield "grows large and bears good crops without being hoed"—one simply girdled the trees, made a deep incision encircling the trunk, then waited upon them to die, meanwhile poking holes in the ground into which one dropped the seed.

The men departed Wakefield on horseback, riding through "red oak, beech, maple, pine, and hemlock"; upon Cutler's recommendation they snacked upon "a great plenty of the Imperial raspberry." The trail soon took a steep descent to a lazy brook upon which was an abandoned beaver dam that was sufficiently strong to serve as a bridge. "It was old," Cutler wrote, "and the sticks so nearly rotten we could not see them. It appeared like a mill-dam with some quantity of earth thrown up." They crossed the rapid but low Pine River, which their horses navigated scarcely better than they did the road, which was itself "exceedingly uneven, in some places very rocky, with sharp hills." The few settlements they passed when they emerged from the surrounding forest were "indifferent," unlike the landscape to the north, painted with the "tall and straight" Norway and white pines as well as birch and oak, with hazy hills and bald mountains forming the background. The road took them over "Seagel's hill, from whence we had a very grand opening to the N., presenting to view distant ridges of very high mountains, rising behind each other, the farthest supposed to be the White Mountains," at least according to their guide Place. But Belknap was not so sure; "the air being hazy, [they] could not certainly determine." When they arrived at Captain Brown's at the small settlement of New Garden, a gentle, cool breeze blew from the south and the smell of pine was overwhelming.

The next morning, after the men awoke at 4:30, and while they prepared for the journey, they spoke briefly with Captain Brown, who told them he had come to this "New Garden," as he called it, four years earlier, during wartime, had "built a house and barn, and cleared ninety acres of land" from the surrounding forest of "beech, maple, and pine." The soil was "light and sandy," hence not very productive. It was a seven-mile journey to Great Ossipee Pond. At this crossroads George Place told them to expect a stage that would take them to

Eaton. While they waited they explored, swam in the pond, fished "using whortleberries and blue-berries" with great success, ate blueberries, and drank rum and water. The horses ate from an "oat-trough" kept in readiness for the stage. The road passed along the southern and eastern shores of the pond; the sandy shores reminded Cutler of familiar beaches along the Massachusetts north shore. The pond was broad and quiet; forest surrounded it; the mountains loomed above the trees, "grand ranges . . . arising one above another. [Mount] White-face was in plain sight." The stage took them upon a strong, extensive bridge that crossed the exiting Ossipee River on its journey east to the Saco. Jacob Scadgel was the builder in 1773. *"The Ossapy River,"* Belknap wrote in his journal, *"runs out of the pond, first northerly, then turns easterly, under a large mountain in Effingham . . .* called . . . Green Mountain." At the north side of the pond they discovered the remains of the fort that Captain John Lovewell had built before his disastrous march against the Pequawket Indians almost sixty years before. From here the stage pursued a northern course, following in the distant wake of Lovewell; after a few miles the stage departed a different way than to Eaton. On horseback again, Cutler complained that the remaining "five miles" to Eaton was "over pitch and Norway-pine plains, with very low shrubs, sweet fern, and brakes; very hot and tedious." Some diversion was provided by sporadic beaver ponds and meadows forming the foreground to the constant view of forests and hills. At Eaton, awaiting another stage to take them to Conway, they rested and supped. The town was "very poor" with but a few "miserable huts, on . . . rocky, rough land, constantly uphill and down." One Dr. Jackson, originally from Rochester, and his sons operated what amounted to a tavern at the stage-stop. It was "a most wretched place indeed": the log house was "low" and "poor . . . with stones roughly thrown together for a chimney." Jackson and his neighbors kept continual fires burning in the pastures to defend their livestock from the on-slaught of the bloodthirsty mosquitoes. The hosts had only bread for the meal, to which the journeyers contributed "our

*Ossipee Valley*. For early explorers the Ossipee Valley heralded the coming beauty and danger of the distant White Mountains.

fish and pigeons," caught and shot at Ossipee Pond; "with pork and bacon fried up in one mess, we made a most sumptuous dinner."

On the stage to Conway, six miles north of Eaton, the men witnessed a transformation from "miserably barren" land and impoverished people to fruitful soil farmed by well-fed inhabitants who lived in "well built houses." They left the stage and mounted their horses in a shower of rain at one Abbot's after a brief meal that featured "new potatoes, about one-half grown." Abbot told Belknap that only within a fortnight had the snow completely disappeared from the mountains. The three miles to McMillan's Tavern included two river crossings, the Swift and Saco, both of which were low, in places rocky and barren of water; speckled rocks of varying hues glistened beneath the surface of the clear, cold streams; the Saco gurgled sweet music. Pillars and cylinders of clouds rose and fell in the humid air; sunshine bathed surrounding peaks. "These scenes have a most agreeable effect," the men agreed. The intervales formed by the Saco were rich and fertile hills rising from the river; crops dotted the landscape. One farmer greeted the travelers and, hearing that a historian was among them, informed Belknap of the remains of "two Indian forts" nearby.

McMillan's Tavern was the agreed-upon rendezvous. The locals considered McMillan's farm, situated just north of Conway on the way to the mountains, to be the *doorway to the white hills*. John Evans frequently came this way and knew McMillan well. Originally from Ireland, Andrew McMillan immigrated to Penacook, New Hampshire, during the 1750s to find the colony embroiled in war against France. Like Evans, McMillan found Robert Rogers' appeal for men too good to resist. He served Rogers faithfully as a lieutenant; for his work the Crown awarded McMillan a grant of several hundred acres in the upper Saco Valley. Having been a storekeeper in Penacook, he moved his operations to Conway in 1774 before the war. By then he had risen to the rank of colonel in the local militia. Hunters and settlers stopped at McMillan's for a warm bed, food, and supplies before beginning the long ascent to the mountains and the Western and Eastern notches over twenty miles distant.

The journeyers entered into "a fine house" highlighted by a large room where the thick smell of ale and stew greeted their noses. A roaring fire and candles broke the darkness. Mc-Millan typically hailed his visitors with the husky voice of his homeland—as a result many of his guests thought his name was *McMullen*. The hungry scientists and clergyman wolfed down a plentiful meal of "full-grown cucumbers . . . peas, lamb," and maple syrup. Outside was a hard rain and an early dusk; the air was abnormally cool. Colonel Whipple and Captain Evans, already arrived through pre-arrangement and fed, joined the others for after-supper planning of the next day's journey.

The morning of Friday, July 23, was fair after a night of showers; the air remained cool. The expedition created quite a stir in Conway, as it had in Eaton, among people who rarely saw more than one or two travelers pass through—and these were usually hunters. The simple farm folk had a good laugh at the expense of the men, who appeared to be going off to war, marching as they did with guides and axe-men, armed with rifles and other instruments, sextants, barometers, thermometers—all very large, "slung across" their backs. Some of the "good women" of Conway understandably empathized with the scientists and their weapons and instruments, knowing that they were headed for Passaconaway's realm. The locals frequently heard the *strangeness in the air*, saw the odd lights, felt the chill of ghostly apparitions. They seriously asked the clergymen Belknap, Cutler, and Little to use their power to call upon the angels of God to "lay the spirits" of the Great Mountain, to free the honest farm people from Passaconaway's curse. Their credulity horrified Belknap, while it amused the quiet Evans, who was used to such talk.

The weather was mild, the day partly cloudy—perfect for travel. Horses stamped the ground impatiently. The men, likewise, were filled with expectation. Captain Evans mounted, looked to see the others waiting, then with a silent gesture of command set out. The journey into the wilderness had begun.

The men rode single file on what remained of the Shelburne Road, which Belknap described as "now grown up with bushes as high as a man's head on horseback, full of wind-fallen trees, deep mires, and broken bridges; and in one place a tornado had so torn up the trees that we laboured with excessive difficulty to get through with our horses." Evans frequently had to dismount and wield the axe to clear a path. The road paralleled the east side of the southward-flowing Saco. The Green Hills loomed to the right; Moat Mountain dominated to the left, across the river. After traveling two miles they reached the confluence of the Saco, Ellis, and the East Branch of the Saco, the latter of which they forded. Kearsarge Mountain loomed above them. For the next hour they followed the Ellis and the ascending landscape until they came to a likely spot in a green valley where a mountain brook entered the Ellis. This future site of the town of Jackson was the home and lands of one Benjamin Copp, who had moved his family there in 1778. The land remained the same as when he first arrived: the wilderness was reluctant to yield a garden. Copp, his wife, and his children were suspicious of the armed travelers and clearly interested in their hasty departure. The scientists tarried for half an hour, strolling, baiting and watering their horses, and expressing their amazement at what lay before them.

There stood the Great Mountain. It "appeared," Belknap wrote in his journal, "like a naked rock, of its proper grey color, inclining to brown, the channels where water descends plainly discernible, being whiter than the rest." Belknap peered through the telescope, then shared the view with the others: Cutler, Little, Whipple, and Dr. Joshua Fisher. Manasseh Cutler and Joshua Fisher had for years been fast friends: they shared an interest in science and medicine, particularly botany, and both men contributed to scientific, philosophical, and medical organizations. As young men living in Dedham, Massachusetts, they formed the "Thursday Night Club" to share books and ideas. Fisher started practicing medicine at

Ipswich at the same time that Cutler settled with the First Parish of the same town. After 1773 Fisher lived in nearby Beverly and the two men remained active friends. While Cutler served as a chaplain during the war, Fisher, newly married, served on a privateer that was captured by the British. Fisher eluded his captors, however, and escaped from England across the channel to France, where he found a friendly ship to bring him home. Fisher was not completely content with the practice of medicine, which was one reason for his journey to the mountains. Another reason was his suspicion that such a journey might be good for his health. Besides a terrible speech impediment, he thought himself consumptive, except that rather than losing weight he was gaining it. Despite his apparent struggle with asthma, Fisher prepared to enter into what he knew could be a dangerous environment for his health—he rather hoped the effect would prove salutary.

Departing Copp's, Evans led the men north-northwest along the road. Having heard that Evans had ascended the Great Mountain in 1774, Belknap rode alongside the pilot and peppered him with questions. Evans told the portly scientist about the impacted snow on the south side of the mountain, which set Belknap's mind in motion. "If so vast a quantity of snow lodges and remains on the White Mountains," he remarked in his journal, "how many more mountains are there towards the N.W. whose frozen summits give the keenness to the wind"? Responding to the belief of nearly two centuries that distant northern lakes send the cold north wind, Belknap argued: " 'Tis not the lakes nor the forests that make the N.W. winds so piercing, but the hoary tops of infinite ranges of mountains, some of which, at the remotest regions, may retain the snow undissolved through the year."

Belknap began to realize that Evans, who had neither the training nor the proclivity to be a scientist, yet who had an intuitive, subjective, practical approach toward nature, was nevertheless a superb source of information that could not otherwise be deduced by using traditional scientific methods. It was from Evans that Belknap saw how a frontiersman bivouacked in the forest; learned how wilderness roads were built; realized how hunters could keep their bearings in the forest without a magnetic compass; heard how the hunter constructed a culheag; and witnessed how the least scientific of men could make accurate forecasts of the weather by using the changing temperatures and movements of clouds in the mountains as an almanac, as it were, to predict meteorological events.

It was a fine day, with a bright sun and a calm wind, yet the men cursed the flies and mosquitoes. Horse's hooves thudded on the soil layered with dried pine needles. The dense forest, predominantly hemlock, enveloped them. It was a trail masquerading as a road that tested Evans' expertise as a guide. Sometimes even he was unsure what was road and what was but an animal trace. The Ellis, fortunately, had not noticeably changed in ten years. With such a foundation for bearings, it was improbable that they would become lost. Besides, the man who had nosed his way to safety from St. Francis when others of Rogers' rangers had lost their way and perished, the man who was a crafty old road builder who knew best his old friend the axe, was not the type to get lost.

Three miles upriver from Copp's, Evans led them across the Ellis. Mountains of three thousand feet loomed to the west, south, and east. Mountains of four thousand feet stood to the west-northwest. Mountains of five thousand feet—and higher—soared almost due north. Near the confluence of the Ellis with the New River they arrived at a spectacular, primordial signature of the divine. Rushing water leapt from a height of one hundred feet and soared beautifully downward to a turquoise pool. A wonderfully cool spray wetted he who approached the foot of the fall on a slippery ledge of rock. The New River, created by an autumn freshet in 1775, and the Ellis River revealed at their juncture a particularly violent history of a one-time, thunderous, terrifying wall of water crashing down from above, overwhelming all, alive or dead, in its path, sweeping mangled trees and errant boulders away mercilessly and effortlessly. The scientists studied the remains of this massive, uncontrollable monster. Cutler wrote: "From toward the [Great] mountain above, at the distance of seventy or eighty rods from the top of the cascade, large stones appeared to have been brought down by the water, breaking off large trees at the height of a man's head; breaking the trunks in short pieces, the ends of which were shivered into small splinters, and wedged in among the rocks. In one place the trunks of large trees were curiously lodged in the form of a circular dam, by being stopped by the stumps, nearly as high as a man's shoulders, and filled up above with large rocks of circular form, some small, and others nearly of a ton's weight—perhaps more." Daniel Little, upon inspecting the river, thought that it was of such a force as "to carry a sawmill." The water had a brown, rusty color, which upon tasting proved to be iron. The scientists wanted very much "to explore the [New] river thoroughly," but Evans requested that they keep to their course along the Ellis—the notch was but a short journey ahead.

By late afternoon they reached a spectacular meadow surrounded by towering mountains. The men looked about in amazement, speechless. It was the home of giants: the soft meadow their beds, the walls of rock enclosing a room of open-skied ceiling. The Great Mountain towered above them, its face lined with distant rivers, clothed in the verdure forest. Shadows of clouds spotted the massive mountain sides. Clouds revealed then hid several peaks and ridges that all appeared to be united as one broad summit.

Evans picked a campsite at the edge of the trees near the confluence of several springs falling from the mountain and emerging from the meadow—the source of the Ellis River. He directed the building of a hut while the scientists loitered about, making observations. Belknap and Little explored the meadow and "took a view of the Mountain, which appeared in two very high peaks and several ridges, one of which was bare." Belknap scratched two hasty portraits with a pencil on two large pieces of paper he carried. One had the beginnings of a map of the environs encompassing the White Mountains, which included rivers, mountains, markers, and the path of the journeyers. The other was a clear sketch of "the appearance of the great White Mountain from the meadow at its foot." The sketch illustrates the tree line, the gulfs and ridges of the mountain, and its highest summit, looking like a sugar loaf.

Meanwhile as the light of day vanished Evans directed Place, Wingate, the two students Bartlett and Hubbard, and a servant of Joseph Whipple whose name is unknown, to gather firewood and hemlock branches full with the soft needles. Taking his axe Evans found and cut down three birch saplings six feet high and stripped them of bark. Making sure that the saplings had forked ends, he sharpened the opposite ends and plunged them six feet apart into a patch of soft, moist soil that was flat and elevated slightly above surrounding ground. Next he took a long birch pole of about twelve feet and laid it perpendicular to the standing poles in their crotchets. Then he took a number of stout switches, six to seven feet in length, and laid them from the horizontal pole to the ground, forming a triangular frame. He took the peeled birch bark and laced it in and out of the several switches in the form of shingles to make a secure ceiling. With the hemlock branches Evans formed a carpet on the hut floor that would give to the weight of the twelve men. The opening of the hut was leeward, and as the wind was from the northwest, the back of the hut was to the mountain. The smoke from their fire would blow away from the opening yet still provide radiant heat, light, and protection during the night. Evans' hut fascinated Belknap, who heard the frontiersman comment that he himself needed no such convenience but had built it for the comfort of the scientists.

Whipple, declaring his intention to take a bearing on the Great Mountain, strolled to the meadow with Belknap in tow. The mountain lay west-northwest, bearing 280 degrees from magnetic north. The sun was setting when Belknap, returning to the hut, "fell into a deep hole full of water." Wet and cold, wrapped in a blanket, he lay down next to the fire. Belknap recalled later having "shifted as well as I could, but received so much damage from this accident that I was ill all night."

Sundown. Having tied their horses "by the head," the men lay down in a row, wrapped in their blankets, their feet warmed by the fire. The night was cool, rainy, and breezy. The rain pattered on the hut ceiling. Tall pines crashed in the wind, which even shrieked at times. Belknap, "feverish and weak," bone-weary, had difficulty sleeping. At such times the world of dreams counters reality, which is dark and confused. Nightmarish thoughts and anxieties dominate the imagination, so that one might hear many things, see images in the night; and the past, others' haunting memories, stories of the strange and supernatural, became a little more believable.

Morning. The day dawned fair upon the mountain wilderness. The images of the night slowly faded as the reality of the Great Mountain, looming above, began to dominate. New sunlight sought to pierce the white vapors hovering atop the mountain. Each explorer prepared for the ascent in his own way, with his own thoughts. The mountain silently beckoned. Its passive strength challenged those with the strongest wills to scale its vast stillness, its vast quiet, to bring movement to emptiness, sound to silence. Barren yet full, like man, the mountain's greatness depended on human feelings of awe and wonder. The mountain's significance lay in the challenge. All journeyers, past and present, stand at the base of the unknown and feel the pull toward the summit. Questions begin early in man: questions of life and meaning. Men look to the mountain for knowledge, and with each step they move toward an answer. The terra incognita of men's minds is deep and infinite, yet so too is the quest to know. This summer day in 1784 was a part of the endless continuum of ignorance and knowledge, of fear and will, of the challenge and the attempt. Quietly, then, the explorers prepared for the Unknown.

They set out just after six o'clock. Evans, who took the lead, dressed in buckskin; the others had, perhaps, linen shirts and wool breeches with leather boots to their knees. Most wore coats, expecting cold at the summit. Armed with rifles and a pistol, they also carried "1 sextant, 1 telescope, . . . 2 surveying compasses," and a single barometer and thermometer. Since the beginning of the journey Cutler had rarely spent an hour at rest from worry over his barometers and thermometers, of which he had two of each at the start. His intention had been to keep a daily journal of the weather, especially temperature changes; this task he had faithfully done, notwithstanding the loss of one thermometer. He would be frustrated, however, in another of his goals: to determine the height of the mountain by measuring barometric pressure. Unfortunately the bumps and grinds of the journey rendered one of the barometers useless; nevertheless Cutler determined to make do with the other. If he could not use two—place one at the base, the other at the summit, record the drop in atmospheric pressure conforming to the mountain's height, and calculate the resultant altitude—he could at least attempt his calculations with one and hope for the best. Barring bad weather, Cutler intended to use the sextant to determine the precise latitude of the mountain. And more. He had a journal to record data on the mountain flora and a satchel to collect specimens. He had hypothesized that the cold regions of the mountain would yield a distinct, indeed unique, form of plant life; he was later to prove his assumption correct.

Captain Evans proposed to lead the men up the east slope, paralleling a descending mountain brook, on "*a ridge which is one continued ascent* to the top." This has been his route ten years before. He doubted the capacity of some of the men to reach the top, said nothing, but relentlessly pushed them on from the start. His employers had lauded the clear day over breakfast, but Evans was not so sanguine. Haste and good marching order were imperative.

At first, the climb seemed easy. Evans followed an old deer trace that meandered amid the tall trees next to a descending stream that, because of Cutler's interest in halting to examine it and his frustration at being persuaded to the contrary, they christened "Cutler's River." Another nearby brook, which the scientists briefly studied, had "a frothy scum, which . . . proved to be saponaceous," soapy tasting. Fisher, "at the first steep ascent . . . finding a pain in his side, which disabled him, returned to the camp" to join Whipple's servant. Belknap, "being very corporlant" in Little's words, huffing and puffing and seeing in Fisher's fate his own, refused to give in and dragged himself up fifteen hundred feet over two hours of climbing. He alone seemed to require continual rest breaks; the others were anxious to proceed at each unscheduled stop. "Having risen many very steep and extremely difficult precipices," Belknap confessed to his journal, "I found my breath fail." Evans informed the exasperated scientists that they "were not more than half way to the Plain."

Before him, the mountain was the grandest thing in view. As such it became an immediate challenge to Belknap, as it would to any man who sees in the mountain all that he lacks. To ascend it is to scan the earth, to see what few men see, to breathe air few men breathe. To ascend it is to know it, to possess it, to conquer it, to raise oneself to a higher plane, to surpass the limitations of human strength and longevity— to stand at the peak of the world, to touch the marrow of the clouds, to experience the beginning of time. Surely night never falls to dull such a vision. There is a timelessness at the peak: one becomes an Olympian scoffing at the time-world below. The view from the Great Mountain—of the forests, the sea, valleys, and other mountains—is changeless, lasting. How the spirit soars when one can gaze upon the earth, dominate it with one's eyes, feel what the mountain feels!

But Belknap could see for himself that the distance to "the summit . . . appeared much higher than the distance we had come." It appeared an even "steeper" route as well: "The clouds were covering the mountain above us." All appeared daunting. Belknap, exhausted and a bit worried, "persuaded" himself that "if I got to the top I should be fit for nothing but to lie down and sleep." The men huddled on the trail and collectively decided that Belknap must return, which he did in a good-natured way, refusing the several offers to accompany him back to camp, calling out to the men as he descended: *"In magnis voluisse sat est"* (To be willing is noble enough).

Belknap descended alone, but not in defeat, rather continued astonishment. Human success or failure is meaningless next to the wonder and beauty of "elder Scripture." With Cutler's River to guide him, Belknap could hardly get lost. So instead of worrying about the trail, or the aches of his body, he reveled in the Creation and betook himself to exploration. His eyes directed away from the ever-present summit, he could see the smaller miracles and less visible jewels of nature. Spying a distant wall of granite, he strayed from the trail long enough to investigate. It was "about *five feet high, and twelve or fifteen long*, composed of square-faced stones, laid as fair and regular as a piece of masonry." Belknap approached the wall from above, gingerly tread down one side, then came out in front. He heard a delightful singing, then discovered its source: a trickle of fresh, sweet water glistened from the stone, tempting the thirsty explorer. He sat and rested, feeling a sublime euphoria, knowing that he was perhaps the first man to worship at this temple.

Belknap had been in the forest many times; always he had the same feelings. He felt wonderfully alone amid so many facets of life, so much diversity, the abundance of nature. Here he felt the perfect mixture of humility and dignity, of significance and insignificance. He was amid something unfathomable, yet he knew himself a part of it. He sensed a beauty unrevealed to his senses, a perfection unknown to the ignorant. He looked about him and contemplated the whole. The forest mocks the man who would ignore the whole of creation and confine his attention to himself. So might the solitary rock appear eternally independent in its immovable location. Yet after many years the wind brings a visitor, a seed, and deposits it next to the rock. The seed takes root and grows, steadily, while the rock continues in apparent sameness. Soon the tree matures and its roots spread outward, first conquering the underlying soil, then the rock itself. As the years pass the tree's "roots either penetrate" the rock's crevices "or run over its surface." Time passes. Moss forms on the tree, and "assumes a grotesque appearance, hanging in tufts, like long hair, from the branches"; as it grows it soon touches, then covers, the rock "like a carpet." The rock exists, to be sure, but only as the tree exists. Neither is singular; each shares the other.

Belknap reached camp about ten o'clock. "The ascent was too much a strain on my thorax," he told a surprised Fisher. Belknap, "though much fatigued," told Fisher of his discoveries as well as a theory he was developing in the wake of his experiences. "The side of the Mountain . . . is composed of a mass of loose rocks, covered with a deep green moss, in some places as thick as a bed. The moss covers the rocks and then interstices, so that in many places you walk on it and it bends under you, and yet supports your weight; but in other places it proves treacherous, and lets you through, to the danger of your shins." Recalling William Stark's theory about mountain moisture of ten years before, Belknap found confirming evidence that the "moss . . . serves as a sponge to retain the vapors which are continually brought by the winds in the form of clouds against these Mountains, and there deposited." Belknap correctly guessed the continuous source of mountain springs in air rushing against and up these heights, cooling, condensing into clouds, then releasing moisture. He was thoughtful yet exhausted. After "some refreshment," he "slept for two or three hours."

The mountain had retired two men: would there be others? As the sun of mid-morning began to appear after its long concealment behind hills and forest, the winding trail became steeper. Beech, maple, and birch grew less prominent compared to the conifers—pine, spruce, and hemlock. The trail continued rocky and fatiguing through the coniferous forest for another hour until they approached the tree line, the limits of what Cutler would designate the *first zone.* Thereafter they encountered a dense growth of dwarf trees, *krummholz,* stunted by their continual subjugation to the brisk mountain winds. The trees, which ranged from "two to ten feet high," posed a particular challenge to the men, who were unsure whether to slither under on their bellies or leap from tree to tree like acrobats. Evans' quip that he wished for his snow-shoes, though tinged with humor, failed to relieve their fatigue. The intense labor was short-lived. At 10:30, "about two thirds of our way up the mountain," they reached "the clear, as it is called, which is above the trees." Here, "short moss and grass" of the *second zone* replaced the large beds of krummholz. The mountain surface was stone, its crevices harboring "various kinds of vegetables, most of them such as we had never before seen." The botanist Cutler engaged in a veritable clinic, especially with the two Harvard students, Bartlett and Hubbard, examining, picking, tasting, observing, describing, and collecting various berries, "the Labrador tea, of a very aromatic taste and smell," and "a flower resembling the narcissus, the smell agreeable." Wonderfully weak and lonely shrubs contorted into unimaginable positions, but a few inches in height though many more if straightened, intrigued both teacher and students, who wrote: "Among the rocks were spruces about 3 or 4 inches high, which had been perhaps growing several 1000 years to obtain this height; the winds and snow had kept their tops even with the surface of the rocks, which made them appear as though they had been mowed and frequently sufficiently firm to support us as we walked upon them."

The angle of ascent steepened as Evans led them on an hour's climb over huge boulders that masqueraded as the steps of giants—such was Daniel Little's opinion. Cutler, however, argued that "they are without the least appearance of regularity, and were evidently washed bare by the descent of large torrents of water occasioned by the dissolving of the snow." During this part of the ascent a "curious scene" fascinated the students. They witnessed the formation, movement, and dissipation of clouds that drifted and swayed in "delightful confusion." It was a unique experience to walk among the clouds and to survey them from on high. "The sun at the same time shining clear upon their upper surfaces" exhibits "a curious appearance." When they reached the first summit a little before noon "the heavens" were "clear," if hazy; they realized they were enjoying "certainly one of the most extensive prospects that any part of New England exhibits." Neighboring summits appeared less profound than their distance and danger would otherwise suggest. The words the men used to describe the scene were simple, childlike. Great peaks looked like molehills and hay-cocks. Rivers appeared to be trickles of water after a summer storm. Lakes were puddles. To traverse massive ridges seemed but a walk in the park.

The men felt a strange power as they surveyed the earth, the power that comes from awareness of the ignorance and blindness of one's normal existence, where one cannot see beyond the next ridge and so must guess at the lay of the land and wonder about its inhabitants. The men felt the power of a broadened vision, a perspective beyond self, the power of the ages, of the passage of time condensed into the single moment. Theirs was an individual, unique experience that was nevertheless felt by all, a shared singularity. And within them stirred odd feelings of warmth and loneliness, fascination and fear, power yet weakness, life yet death. These strange sensations could hardly have been expressed by John Evans, much less the scientists Cutler and Little. Such feelings derived from the primitive sensation of being alone with Creation, the nascent world at birth. Each man could sense divinity, could sense an inscrutable order and plan. Along with such grand and sublime feelings came others, feelings of smallness, of insignificance. The men felt the humility of ignorance as well as the exhilaration of recognition—the knowledge of self, of God, that rushes in from the northern hills, brought by the wind. Piety is one's only response.

Narrowing their vision, the men spied distant summits of the White and Green mountains, descending rivers such as the Androscoggin and Ammonoosuc, distant ponds and lakes such as Lake Champlain, and the broad Atlantic as well. Little noted that "the houses upon the Connecticut river open to

view with the naked eye." Cutler, fascinated by the scene below his feet, commented on the lack of plant life on the initial
summit. This was his *third zone*, "above the limits of vegetation." Turning their attention to the Sugar Loaf, the party
began the ascent. "We were an hour and twenty-one minutes
walking from the first summit to the pinnacle of the Sugar-
loaf, and had the best walking of any part of our journey from
the bottom of the mountain."

Upon reaching the highest peak the wind was fierce and
cold beyond their expectations. The roar of distant lands and
summits, the story of the wind, filled their ears. While some
stood in wonder and peace examining the "grand prospect," a
"horizon" that ranged perhaps "400 miles," Cutler set about
to measure what he could. But "before we had time to make
any of those observations and measurements respecting distant objects, for which purpose we had been at pains of carrying proper instruments to this height of atmosphere, we had
the mortification to be involved in a dense cloud." Cutler, engaged in the vain hope that it would eventually clear, took the
pains to hang his thermometer and barometer by "two
walking-sticks." The thermometer, which he carried up the
mountain inside his "winter baize jacket with sleeves, a thick
broadcloth jacket, and . . . greatcoat," read "120–128 degrees
above fever heat." In the open air the mercury soon dropped
to 44 degrees. He took a barometer reading of "22.60, which
will give 9,000 feet for the height of the mountain." Meanwhile the cloud thickened, making the use of the sextant to
take the latitude a useless enterprise.

The windblown fog was "as cold as November." The men
stayed as long as they could on the summit, dining "on par-
tridges and neat's tongue." Evans found the hat he had left
behind in June 1774. Little began to chisel *NH* into a rock,
but his frozen hands forced him to turn the job over to Whipple. Cutler found that, against his will, "my teeth chattered
most violently in my head, and I felt a universal rigor, which
so affected my arms and hands that, when I repacked my thermometer and barometer, I had almost lost the use of my fin-

gers." He later blamed this on "the profuse sweats we had undergone in our ascent." Different men attempted to carve their names in the rock even though they had brought a sheet of engraved lead that answered the very purpose—they deposited the lead with Evans' hat under a rock and prepared to depart.

Unfortunately the fog played havoc with the compasses and was so thick that no one was certain of directions. Evans, who was used to such weather, favored waiting out the fog that upon clearing would reveal the path. Arguments ensued between the scientists and Evans and among Evans, Place, and Wingate. "The cold was now so intense" and the scientists' discomfort so extreme that they "insisted" that the "guides . . . make an attempt" to descend. Everyone thought that they knew the correct path. One, then another, claimed the lead. At such times John Evans was at his best. He refused to pass command to another and quickly reestablished his authority. But what was the right way? Some unthinking men in desperation would plunge forward disregarding the path just to get out quickly. Others, scientists, would try to retrace the immediate past, gauge the wind, examine the landscape, look for footprints, any concrete sign that would appear to the senses to help one deduce the truth. John Evans chose a third option: the intuition of the moment.

John Evans did not use maps. He felt his way through the forest and up the Great Mountain, following rivers and animal traces, moss on trees, the location of the sun. He had been in such situations before, without a compass or map, lost, among concerned and anxious comrades. Evans had learned patience. He knew how to adapt to the exigencies of a situation, to take from his surroundings the means to live, to grasp opportunity from a given moment, to fight fear and go steadily onward, to act on hunches and instinct when lacking ready proof, to rely on quiet sensations and the subtle hints of the forest, to blend in like the camouflaged deer and the leaves rustling in the wind. He knew how to imitate the wilderness to take from it the means of survival.

Cutler's account reveals that on the shrouded summit the frightened scientists grew impatient with the cautious Evans, who was uncertain yet also unafraid. Evans' hesitancy derived from the fleeting moment of weighing options before proceeding with diligence notwithstanding future possibilities. Evans personified the wilderness, that timeless experience of the singular moment, the instinctual present, the unplanned action. He represented the anonymous, initial explorer, he who is the harbinger of civilization, behind whom comes the much-heralded, well-known scientist, journalist, publicist, follower. The scientist who loses his way has not followed proper procedure and methodology, has not correctly used available instruments and technology. The intuitive wilderness explorer such as John Evans loses his way as a matter of course—to lose one's way in the wilderness is the only way to find the correct path, to forge a course into the unknown that others may follow. The prerequisite of the scientist is the established existence of the path, which has been set forth by another, the wilderness hunter, trapper, and axe-man, who is always on the verge between knowledge and ignorance, who is always on the frontier of science.

Evans guessed the route of return, leading the men through the icy fog that grew thicker as they descended the Sugar Loaf. Upon reaching the initial summit, they were wet and cold, fatigued and thirsty. They found a small creek with fresh, cool water. Proceeding, descending into the unknown, the way grew steeper, more treacherous. "Our prospect was so bounded by the density of the cloud that we could see but a few feet . . . before us, and therefore apprehended no great danger in attempting to descend it, which appeared absolutely necessary, as we could see no way to avoid it." Had it been clear, they would have never tread this way. As it was, the blind leading the blind by intuition, they crawled down a cliff holding on by their hands, fixing their heels in the rock, with each uncertain step trying not to plummet from what could be a sheer cliff. Notwithstanding the danger the men were "cheerful" because of "the novelty of traveling in the clouds, and the hope that we should not be totally lost in them." They were, nevertheless, completely lost, and Evans knew it. The slope and footing grew so dangerous he decided it was best to reconnoiter to see if he was right in assuming that this path led to danger rather than safety. Evans told the others to wait; he would return momentarily. He descended into the clouds and disappeared. The men waited "some time for his return to us," then grew impatient. One then another called out to Evans: What is the situation? Shall we advance or retreat? No answer. The depths of the fog stared back; all was silent. Cutler inched to the front of the line and called repeatedly, cupping his hand to his ear and looking intently into nothingness. All he could see was a "horrid precipice, and it appeared to me that no person could go any further without great hazard to his life. We were now in a sad dilemma"—lost, stuck in the fog on a mountain precipice, wet, cold, and leaderless. "Our guide, we concluded, was either killed, stunned, or had received some kind of disaster which rendered him unable to answer us. It was not possible for us to go to him, and it was doing great violence to our feelings to think of leaving him without knowing any thing of the condition he was in." Where was John Evans?

Chapter Five

# PLUNGE INTO THE PAST

Captain John Evans entered into the eerie void, each hesitant step penetrating the silence, forging a path into a realm of darkness, Passaconaway's realm. He left the men to reconnoiter, carefully placing the heels of his boots in the small platforms of stone. He had guessed right—the way was too treacherous. As he put his foot down a stone gave way. He tried to regain his grip but could not. Falling forward, he reached out, grasping the wind. He rolled and smashed, turning over and over, spiraling down into the abyss. When would he lose contact with loose earth and rocks and soar through empty space, a free fall that would never end? His axe, which he held in his hands, he threw before him, freeing his hands to grab, to pummel the rock for a ledge, a hold to halt his sliding. He hit hard a solid, sloping platform and came to rest. A shower of stones and pebbles, a miniature avalanche, rained down upon him. Having entered into light from the dark void, Evans looked around to see that he was out of the fog. The tree line was below. Gingerly gathering his wits, he inched toward a makeshift path that led to sloping yet stable ground. He had no idea how far he had come, nor whether the others would soon follow.

As he was assessing his options, Evans heard a voice from above, coming from the fog. It was someone "hallooing"—it sounded like Colonel Whipple. Evans shouted that he was roughed up but able to move, that it was too dangerous for the others to follow, that they should find an alternate route. He would meanwhile, he yelled, descend to the tree line and build a fire, the smoke and light of which would serve as a beacon to them. Whipple agreed and Evans heard no more.

Someone, Whipple perhaps, or George Place, took charge. They tried to ascend and retrace the way they had come but the rocks that served so well for heel-holds on the way down did not work for toe-holds on the way up. "In this awful dilemma, one of them spied a cross-gully, which had a more gradual ascent; and in this they got to the plain." Having extricated themselves from the ravine, the journeyers found a ridge to take them down the east side of the mountain. When they got to the tree line it was getting dark. They saw rising smoke in the distance, toward which they went.

The fire was Evans', of course. Having traversed the ravine for an hour, Evans came to the tree line, gathered wood, and prepared to build a fire. With twigs he built a structure that resembled a miniature hut, laying small twigs in a row against a larger stick. Underneath the twigs he piled dried pine needles. Then he patiently struck together the two pieces of flint that he always carried. Random sparks flew; one lone spark nestled in the needles and took hold. Evans let it grow before he gently blew on it, causing the twigs to ignite. He scattered bigger pieces of dried wood, building a sustainable blaze. He carefully laid crosswise large pieces of white birch, building the blaze while producing much smoke. The flames helped counter the utter loneliness he felt. True, he was often alone in the woods hunting and trapping. But his experience on the Great Mountain felt different. He wondered and worried about the others. Would they find an alternate route? Would it be on the east slope, where he thought he was? Would they rendezvous before nightfall? But more, it was hard to get out of his mind nagging memories of the past, of the hapless rangers who dragged the silver Virgin to the Great Mountain, of the stories of terrible hauntings and ghostly vengeance, of the legends of Passaconaway's curse. Where were the rangers when they met their end? Was it anywhere near Evans' current location? Was Evans sure that the stories and legends were just that, fictional fairy tales?

Shrugging off the panic that such thoughts could bring, Evans surveyed the surrounding landscape. Clouds still shrouded the summit. Among the bushes, scattered boulders, and endless forest, he saw a great emptiness. No animals appeared, not even birds. No sign of life. All was silent and still save the leaping flames. Evans squatted before the fire, his back to the peak, his face warm and ruddy as it reflected the orange and blue flames. The fire leapt upward in constant change and movement, contradicting the surrounding quiet of the forest. At such times it is a rare man indeed who can ignore strong feelings and deep thought, deny the temptation to reflect upon what has been, what is to come. Perhaps, then, for a few moments Evans lost himself in the fire and was taken to a different time through the medium of his thoughts.

He thought of the coolness of the October night, made colder by the intense pain of a belly long without food. October becomes November quickly when hunger denies the body warmth. It had been years ago when he was young, though already in his twenties a veteran of war and suffering. He was a ranger. And being a ranger, he was part of a force of others engaged in a contest of wills against the enemy. The contest lasted many years. He had seen his fill of native attacks against New Hampshire frontiersmen, neighbors in scattered towns along the Merrimack River. Why, even Rogers, his friend and captain, had known firsthand the devastating raids of the Indians during the 1740s.

In his mind he saw the infant, the progeny of parents who were members of a tribe, the St. Francis Indians, that in the 1750s few New Hampshirites could contemplate without horror. The tales of Indian barbarity were numerous, of white men and women wishing only to die to release them from the hideous tortures inflicted by their tormenters. But such knowledge could not force Evans to kill a helpless infant, to crush its skull against a tree as so many white children had died at the hands of its people. Yet it was time for retaliation. So, at least, thought Rogers, as well as most of the rangers that October day in 1759 when, after so many years on the defensive, the English took the offensive against the St. Francis tribe. The rangers had inflicted ample destruction on the sleepy Indian village in the early morning hours, and many Indian infants had died already when Evans hesitated to kill the crying one before him. He would never forget Rogers' words as the commander grabbed the child and dashed his head against a hemlock: "Nits will be lice."

Whether or not Evans recalled his years as a ranger while sitting on a lonely mountain side nearly two decades later is indeterminable. Yet his experience as a sergeant in the provincial military band, Rogers' Rangers, during the French-Indian War of the 1750s and 1760s determined the character of John Evans. If he did not daily recall his experiences as a ranger, if they were not always present in his consciousness, nevertheless they formed such a part of him that one could not look upon Evans, nor hear his voice, without those experiences of pain, suffering, death, and comradery that formed the life of a ranger being revealed.

The spirits of the dead later had their revenge, or so it seemed, on the retreat from the destroyed village to safety, two hundred miles south through an unrelenting wilderness. The rangers took what food they could from the village and thought to kill game along the way. But nature intervened to send freezing rain to drive game south, ahead of the retreating, soon starving men. And so the paradox occurred that they should be starving at harvest time. Some bands, such as Evans', returned to civilization. Others vanished, sacrificed either to the violence of pursuing natives, or to the violence of their own pain—the gnawing hunger, the damp cold, the directionless wilderness. Evans and his men survived on the edibles of the stingy October forest. Fire was of little relief to the men; there was no warmth and pleasure in something one could not eat. For two weeks they made their way through mountain notches, forded swollen streams, and waded through murky bogs, driven only by the deep eternal urge to survive. A full month after they departed north from the fort, and three weeks after they destroyed St. Francis, Evans and his men straggled into Fort Number Four on the Connecticut, cold and tired, with a feeling beyond hunger in their guts . . . but alive.

Such was the man who sat beside the fire that beckoned to others who thought of nothing but their own cold and hunger, and who yelled with joy when they saw the distant, rising smoke.

The only fire that Jeremy Belknap, Joshua Fisher, and Whipple's servant looked upon was their own, built as night crept closer and it began to drizzle. The afternoon had been spent at camp; Belknap and Fisher explored the spongy meadow and inspected each of two abandoned beaver dams, situated respectively at the northern and southern edges of the meadow. They examined the source of the northward flowing Peabody River, a tributary of the Androscoggin. They did some bird-watching, too. "As it grew toward night, we secured the horses, picked up wood for our fire, and, it beginning to rain, repaired our tent with bark, took all the baggage into it, anxiously expecting the return of our friends, but they appeared not; we therefore went to rest." Worried about his friends, Belknap's mind wandered. This had been an eventful day for him, one for which he had long planned, one that had not ended as he had imagined. He wondered about his friends and their experiences. Were they at present safe or in danger? And, if the latter, would it not be an acceptable consequence of such an adventure? The price of life is the decay of the body and eventual death. Belknap's struggle on the mountain had been life in miniature: life is wholly comparative; one rarely reaches one's desires. Defeat follows soon upon victory, and victory upon defeat. Death snatches the best of men in the best of health, without warning. Were his friends already in the clutches of darkness? Or were they given a temporary respite from the inevitable? Patience alone is required in such a situation, as in life itself. And with that thought Belknap slept, or at least made the attempt.

The mountaineers, however, enjoyed little sleep that night. Though not in danger, any comfort they took in their safety was reduced by the rain and the cold. They spent the night huddled around the fire, "parboiled and smoke-dried." If Belknap *thought* of patience, these men made the practice of it their supreme activity as they awaited the light of day. Eventually dawn's faint rays greeted their eyes. The rain stopped. The men lost no time in the descent. No record exists to indicate their path. One imagines Evans eschewed the thick forest for the high ground of a ridge, perhaps lying between the two great ravines, Huntington and Tuckerman. They hiked a good four hours. Mosquitoes reveled in the moist and humid weather. The many rodents and other mammals that resided in the northeast mountains stayed out of sight. The still and peace of the distant summit, now bathed in sunlight, countered their memories of the cold fog of yesterday. The men, fatigued, sore, and hungry, took little notice of the surrounding trees, the verdure hemlock and white birch, its bark peeling in places on the trunk, and the many other birches and ashes. Nor were they grateful that the wind, often ferocious, was calm. Nor did they note and study the many birds who nest in the forested slopes of the Great Mountain. The men were quiet, wanting only to reach camp.

By mid-morning Evans and his troop reached level ground. Knowing the camp must be nearby, he fired a rifle, which was momentarily "answered; it was repeated by them once," Belknap wrote, "and by us twice, and they presently arrived safe." The newcomers breakfasted, after which Cutler, taking advantage of the sunshine, "went into the meadow and," using a surveying compass, "took a base and angles to measure the height of that part of the top of the Mountain visible from thence, which is not the highest pinnacle, but a bluff on the eastern side of the Plain." Belknap and Fisher learned about the others' experiences and received a clear account of the summit. It particularly interested Belknap that no pond existed on the summit, confirming Nicholas Austin's account of his 1774 ascent but contradicting the descriptions of the summit found in the accounts of Captain Wells, John Josselyn, and the source of the Neal/Field/Josselyn journey.

Evans' goal was to depart from the meadow following the Peabody River by means of the Shelburne Road, then pick up an old trail that would bring them northwest around the Great

Mountain to Whipple's plantation at Dartmouth. He esti-
mated it at a day's journey but had not counted on the unplanned bivouac on the mountain and the late start in the
morning. It was July 25, the Lord's Day, though the clergymen
had little chance for devotions notwithstanding the great ca-
thedral rising above them. The Peabody cut a path through a
very dense forest. The Shelburne Road had not been used for
seven years, according to the best estimates of Whipple and
Evans. Hence it was "grown up with bushes and filled with
wind-falls, the bridges broke, and the mires deep." Belknap,
who loved to engage in traveler's tales, especially when he had
a ready listener, as was his friend Hazard, wrote a few weeks
later that "the road was worse than what we had travelled on
Friday. The greatest expedition we could make was two miles
in an hour, and in some parts not so much. We kept *one man
before* [Evans], *with an ax, to cut away windfalls, or limbs of
windfalls*, over many of which we leaped our horses, and under many crawled, and went round the tops or roots of many
more, and over many broken or rotten bridges, and through
many deep sloughs." If that description was not enough to
impress Hazard, there was more to tell. "To *aid* the difficulty,
we met with an heavy shower, of two hours' continuance,
which wet us every one to the skin." Fisher, who thought he
might die from such a "shower-bath," bore it cheerfully and
came away with his health intact.

Before the rain they had troubles enough. At some "violent"
moment in the recent past, floodwaters had forced the Peabody to jump its bank and forge a new path. The old bed was
dry. Evans, lost again, had to backtrack and "reconnoiter" a
new route. The men rested while he disappeared for a time
then "returned" with the unfortunate news "that the place
where we should have crossed the river was about 100 rods
back." Once they reached the right road—not the Shelburne
but some other old Indian or deer trace—their pace slowed
considerably to a "rate of a mile and a half an hour," because
it was the most overgrown road one could conceive. Evans

again made much use of the axe while another held his horse. As it grew dark in the early evening they were due north of the Presidentials; Evans guessed they were eight miles from Whipple's. They camped in the middle of the woods near the Moose River, a shallow, beautiful mountain stream filled with fish and tadpoles. The water was sweet and delicious, surrounded by "*wild oats,* which our horses snapt at greedily." Night fell on the fatigued, wet men, who ate a cold dinner and sheltered in a makeshift hut that the resourceful Evans constructed by campfire light. Soon after they bedded down, however, the wind changed, so that the hut's opening was windward. "If we raised our heads a foot from the ground, we were suffocated." The rain continued. Figuring that their horses would stay put, they "*were turned loose into the woods, to brouze the bushes.*" Some of the men made extensive use of rum to help them pass the night. Belknap thought that "chocolate . . . was the best viand" to help him keep "*alive,* I will not say *in spirits.*"

The morning was wet and the men were hungry. But the wonderful fog and silent forest that enwrapped them was astonishing, and their horses were nearby, too. They rode eight miles across "the height of land between Moose River and Israel River," the latter of which had "rich" intervales amid fertile land of tall maple and birch trees. Along the way they had a wonderful view of cloud-capped mountains and saw many culheags, which Evans informed them were "set for sables." Perhaps Evans told the men that such culheags were adapted from Indian models and were only part of the native encyclopedia of woodland lore that hunters such as Evans referenced for survival. More showers wetted them before they reached Whipple's land, heralded by a large manmade opening in the forest.

The cleared land provided a needed respite for tired travelers. Their eyes feasted on the livestock grazing in the clearing, on the fields of corn awaiting harvest, and the garden of vegetables, samples of which, Whipple promised, would dot the table for dinner. Cultivation, the sign of human toil, carving from the wilderness the basis of civilized living, was refreshing indeed.

Whipple's house, toward which they came, was a large structure that substituted ornate eaves and gables for loopholes and heavy bolts. Doors and windows were extra thick, not merely to ward off the cold New Hampshire wind but arrows and gunshot as well. It was a fortress of considerable strength that welcomed them from the wilderness. The plain decorations of the interior appeared luxurious to the travelers. Their dream of preceding days for a fresh change of clothes and a hot meal was answered. As Belknap later told his friend Hazard, "a dry house, a good fire (ay, a *good fire* in the middle of July), and a change of linen, which I had preserved dry in my saddle-bags, was a grand refreshment." Once clean, they feasted on the produce of Whipple's garden.

Colonel Whipple turned out to be a charming host and good storyteller. His graying hair revealed his middle age, but his actions and movements were those of a man at the peak of life's vigor. His long, arched nose dominated an otherwise plain face. His countenance was not unusually distinct or commanding. Nevertheless Joseph Whipple enjoyed command, and enjoyed having an audience.

Notwithstanding sporadic settlement, this north country seemed a raw, untouched land. Early morning mist rolled in and blanketed the land, blinding the observer to its secrets. Great distances appeared within reach, touchable, like the full moon on the horizon. The mysteries of life were there to be found, but where was one to look in the vastness of the mountains? Hence arose stories and legends. Old sailors pointed to the rolling green waves of the sea as the place of mystery. Yet the cloudy verdure of rainy mountains had its own unfathomable deep, its own phantoms and buried treasure, its singular tales of woe. Settlers of the northern frontier such as John Evans knew these tales. Some stories, such as that of the rangers and the silver Virgin, they never tired of telling.

Belknap was all ears—and all eyes. He was astonished and

amazed by all that he heard and saw. The wonder wore off but slowly: he had a full share of it over a fortnight later when he wrote Hazard his impressions of the northern wilderness: "We . . . found ourselves in open ground, in the midst of a vast amphitheatre, surrounded on all sides but the N.W. by cloudcapt mountains. The view was grand. The vapours were rising in innumerable columns from the sides of the mountains, and converging toward their summits, forming into clouds, then descending in showers, after a while reascending as before, and thus keeping up a constant circulation." Belknap wanted to firmly implant the image of the mountains in his mind, so took pencil and paper to draw the seven summits that lay at a great distance before him.

Turning from the sublime to the subtle, Belknap strolled Whipple's lands, like a tourist fascinated by everything and hungry to know. Whipple's tenants told him about the productivity of the rich intervales "formed by the Israel River." He heard about the moose pond a short distance away where the huge animals went "to rid themselves of the flies." There were raspberries aplenty in the forests and orchards already beginning to be weighed down by luscious fruit. Maple was in abundance, and Whipple had an extensive sugaring operation. Workers collected enough sap for a year's supply in March, when conditions were perfect for its collection: clear, cool days and frosty nights, with snow still on the ground. Great iron kettles suspended over bright orange fire boiled the sap to a thick syrup or a tasty crystal. Perhaps Whipple, like most husbandmen, made a deep, V-shaped incision in the tree, from which the sap ran through a small trough to a waiting bucket. Most farmers preserved the tree for annual use by plugging the hole with a stopper. A good tree gave a gallon of sap per day.

The distant peaks bathing in the sunshine of morning vanished during the afternoon of Tuesday, July 27. Storm clouds rolled in to add weight to what could otherwise be a neglected discourse. Belknap, Cutler, and Little held worship services in a barn filled with the stench of hay and manure. Thirty-eight settlers listened to Jeremy Belknap preaching from the first book of Corinthians. The sermon was "the first that ever was preached here." Daniel Little baptized eight children. Manasseh Cutler led them in prayer. The simple farmers emerged from the barn with smiles on their faces and, the clergymen hoped, joy in their hearts.

The clergymen felt joy too, no doubt, joy that there were such people in such a place, braving the challenges of the wilderness, building new lives, opening the door to prosperity, carving a path for posterity. Belknap, the historian of New Hampshire, would one day write detailed accounts of these people. He knew that armed with will, courage, and patience, along with a good horse and an ox or two, a family could in a decade set up a shack and clear some acres, fence the land and sow it, harvest the crop and plant again; live off the land and depend on it; know its ways and tenderly urge it, use it sparingly and thriftily, take from it only what is needed, and never abuse its trust. Only then will the land accommodate the frontiersman and yield its stored plenty.

Everyone dreams of the future. Belknap saw New Hampshire reflected in Dartmouth. He dreamed of towns well set amid cold mountain streams, tall, full forests, and fertile soil. The people are hardworking, rarely contentious, living clean, good, long lives. Largely self-sufficient, yet they have the beginnings of a trade with neighboring towns. Men and women know their respective roles and work in harmony. Men toil on the land; women make the meals and clothes and keep house. Sons and daughters work alongside parents. Home is school. Guns are ubiquitous, as is knowledge of their use, even among women and children. The militia forms the backbone of defense, the backbone of the republic. The people of the republic enjoy all the freedoms and liberties of Americans. Absent from the community are politicians and lawyers—anyone who might disrupt town order. And if the town yet lacks a school, library, or minister, the people have such a regard for learning, for knowledge of nature and God, that such institutions are forthcoming. Such people must think of their children as a plowed field: all that is wanting is seed, sun, and water—

books, instruction, and encouragement. Such a society can be a society of thinkers, seeking practical answers to everyday problems. Thought Belknap, such a society is best fitted for long and lasting happiness.


Morning. The earth was on fire, with hills silhouetted in the bright orange strokes of a new day. Rosy petals of early morning light illuminated the gray, streaky clouds. The Great Artist had been at work; the pastels of the sky betrayed His talent. The men roused with all around them, renewed from the hibernation of the night. Life began anew, and with it the creative energy of its essence. Man and beast live, work, produce, survive in the continual challenge of the day-to-day. As every morning, before and since, the living move to new experiences, new knowledge. But what one goes toward is unknown: the undetermined future. This morning, like all mornings, the demarcation between past and future was abundantly clear. Experience confronts potential and possibility on the line of movement that separates the known from the unknown. *Morning* is a grand metaphor for the journey into the wilderness.

The journeyers departed Whipple's as sunlight set the mountains gloriously ablaze. Joshua Fisher, hoping to collect botanical samples of clear medicinal value, stayed on with his host, Colonel Whipple. Captain Evans led the band of nine south along the Israel River, then through a notch between Pondicherry and Mitten mountains. Several times they crossed the wonderfully cold and fresh Ammonoosuc River on its descent from the mountains to the Connecticut. The Ammonoosuc took them toward the Great Mountain.

The pilot knew the way if no one else did; as they wondered of their path he assured them of his knowledge. For it seemed a great wall barred their way—massive peaks jealously guarded a hidden world. But the axe-man moved onward, and the men followed his makeshift road. Soon the great wall was split in pieces and a corridor opened to their eyes—a never ending tunnel made from the stuff of titans, gorged through great rocky hills. Fiery molten movement, shifting earth, must have made it in a distant era. The place had changed little from a primeval time; it seemed youthful, pure, virginal. It was as God made it. Or, in Little's words, it "is a place, grand and curious, where the Creator has marked a central road through an extensive and fertile country to the provinces of Canada."

Different eyes in different times will view the terra incognita as a land of fascination, potential, or fear. The first whites to set eyes on the notch were involuntary discoverers, captives on their way from hearth, home, and family to French Canada, to live out displaced days at the mercy of the captor. They passed through the notch as they would through fire, with dread, terror, and suffering. Not until 1771 was the notch formally known to the civilized, and then only through the efforts of a solitary explorer. Timothy Nash set out from his home on the Upper Cohos in search of a more convenient route to central and southern New Hampshire. At that time the only known trails from the seacoast to the Upper Cohos were north of the mountains to the Androscoggin, or south to Fort Number Four and then upriver. Legend has it that Nash climbed a tree for a better view; he saw a crease in the mountains and followed it to the notch. The story goes that Nash took news of his discovery to New Hampshire Governor John Wentworth, who offered to make the discoverer a grant of land if Nash could lead a horse through the notch. Nash did and received the land. But more important, the discovery of the notch symbolized the ongoing movement of civilization. What could be next but the building of a road?

Belknap, serving as the eyes for his Philadelphia friend Hazard, reported that the *"Notch"* is "a narrow defile between the Mountains, which rise perpendicularly on the eastern side, and on the other sides in an angle of 45°, forming a bason, in which is an open meadow. . . . The direction of the defile is N. and S. The narrowest part, between two perpendicular rocks, 22 feet, but grows wider as you descend toward the S. The meadow on this height of land *was once a beaver pond, and the damm* yet remains." The scientists, wondering about the origins of the notch, believed it was a visible mark of the Creation and the Great Flood. Cutler, still intent upon his measurements, tried to determine the latitude with the use of the sextant. It surprised everyone to see that a road through the notch was under construction, though no workers were present.

John Evans examined the road. Imagine the expert pacing back and forth in deep consideration: How are the logs cut, and of what length? Is the causeway—formed from the logs laid together, bridging the mud—sufficiently stable to withstand hard rains and the chance freshet? His pacing took him from the meadow, following the causeway south along the east side of the river. He came to one section expertly formed with crushed rock: an expensive undertaking, to be sure, but one that in 1784 New Hampshire could easily afford. Evans knew the man whose confiscated estate financed the road. William Stark was one of Evans' old comrades from the rangers. He and his brother John Stark and Evans had often sat about the campfire telling old stories of hunting incidents and Indian conflicts. John Stark later gained fame for his role at the Battle of Bennington. But William stayed loyal to the Crown. He consequently lost his citizenship, his rights, and his land, four hundred pounds from the sale of which went toward the building of the road that John Evans now studied.

Evans looked from the road, surveyed its surroundings. The road was the only human production in sight. He loved the wildness of the land, loved its savagery. Its challenge stirred him as did nothing else, not the life and death struggle of war nor the challenge of stalking the elusive prey nor the demands of the thick pine on the axe-man's strength and endurance. The wilderness challenge was much simpler. Nevertheless as in war he felt fear: fear of something he was separate from yet a part of, something he sought to control because of being controlled, something outside that should be within. As in the hunt Evans stalked his prey, the wilds—not its individual parts but it as a whole, for the whole is a greater challenge, uncapturable, unconquerable. Evans was a reputable hunter, but this prey was elusive. He could use his will to overcome the strength of a solitary tree. But how can a man cut down a whole forest, or come to know a whole wilderness? He could trek this same circuitous route through the mountains again and again yet still it would be the same elusive region. And still he would try.

The times Evans liked best were times alone in the forest, at work or, better, during the brief pause to catch his breath before continuing the task. That was a time for momentary reflection, when one's body felt alive and one could sense the same in nature. There was an imperceptible feeling of sensuality, of being alone with something one loves, being caressed by the wind, whispered to by the soft sounds of the forest, enveloped in soft arms; the scent was sweet, and one wished never to leave the embrace. One felt drawn to the lover in subtle desire, drawn to a soft and wonderful union of tender love. Neither rapturous nor orgasmic, it was a simple sort of love, easy to engage in, just as easy to leave. Refreshed, relaxed, the task could then be resumed with renewed vigor.

The men had such feelings in the privacy of their own hearts. Only one man, the writer, felt the need to put such feelings to paper. And even Belknap did this rarely. He was more apt to enjoy silently his feelings of love and record only more concrete, objective observations. This is the way of science. But science is easily contradicted in such a place. The wonder and beauty of the craggy summit and solemn notch set his heart pounding, which elicited a response:

The most romantic imagination here finds itself surprized and stagnated! Every thing which it had formed an idea of as sublime and beautiful is here realized. Stupendous mountains, hanging rocks, chrystal streams, verdant woods, the cascade above, the torrent below, all conspire to amaze, to delight, to soothe, to enrapture: in short, to fill the mind with such ideas as every lover of Nature, and every devout worshipper of its Author, would wish to have.

The path from the notch south followed the newborn Saco River as it rose from mountain springs and gained strength

*Saco River.* The valley of the Saco River, which attracted Native Americans and Anglo-Americans alike to build communities along its rich intervales, was the route by which many early explorers penetrated the White Mountain wilderness. *Dartmouth College Library.*

from countless other falling waters seeking the quickest way to the sea. The Saco, *the river*, became the last in a series of metaphors that highlighted, explained, and symbolized the journey into the wilderness. What human thought or action has not been dependent, if only in some vague way, upon the river? Hardly has a human traveled or warred, built or sought food, founded cities or traded, but there has been a river to convey, ascend, descend, cross, divert, bridge, drink from, fish from, sail upon, take water from, live upon. Human history is built upon the flowing waters of the river, a timeless entity nevertheless intricately a part of time. Rushing water comes out of the past, some distant highland, the Mountain, moving toward the future, the Sea. All rivers seem a unity, a whole, until they merge one into another—then they become but a part. One can no more halt the river, no more dam it, than one can dam starlight that comes from a thousand years in the past. The route of the river is millennia old as well, an ancient water-road that symbolizes life, age, diversity, movement, time, existence. It flows in its ancient, hoary path carving elliptic bends, digging away an incalculable time, thrusting before it incalculable dirt, sand, and stone, forging a new path to its destination. Such are the rhythms of the river, staying the same but changing, rising and falling, now dry but in an instant flooded, leaving behind rich silt, soil for the farmer. The river curves amid a mosaic of surrounding hills, lofty overlooks to the water below, as it seeks the quickest descent. The river's apparent efficiency, covering the most ground in the least time, is what attracts the traveler to its banks. The certainty of a river's course, knowing that it has an end, yields security to those who embark upon this watery road. Yet the river is a fickle protector, as apt to destroy as to preserve. Along the path of a particular river at a particular point in time, the weary travelers came seeking the quickest way from the wilderness to civilization.

All nine of the journeyers doubtless agreed with Belknap's lament upon departing the notch: "It was with regret that I left this place and descended toward the south." The path fol-

lowing the Saco took Belknap from a personal spiritual summit to a more mundane reality. He resisted the plummet as
long as he could. "For 2 miles from the summit of this romantic pass the Mountains on each side rise almost, and in
some places quite, perpendicular, and shew several bare and
whitish rocks with polished sides, totally inaccessible. Some
of these, especially when crusted over with ice, may have
given rise to the fable of the *Carbuncle*, with the help of a
little imagination and the reflection of the moon or star
beams." The river tumbled downward, forming rapids and frequent falls; it was noisy, shallow, beautiful. As they traveled
south the mind-boggling cliffs and massive peaks lessened, the
valley widened, fertile intervales took over, and the Saco grew
bold, fed by countless mountain streams, each with its own
singular cascades of wonder. The bookworm Belknap saw a
cliff with *"four large square rocks"* that reminded him of
books on a shelf. Cutler's mind swam as he tried not to drown
in the botanical pool of countless specimens. Little, who
thought of himself as an inventor and engineer, could only
think of the "boldest work of art in New England," the new
road upon which they tread. Evans, freed from the demands of
the axe, looked about and was content to wonder. Still the
pilot, he led the men through a narrow gap under a large rocky
overhang, Sawyer's Rock. Here, he told them that two hunters
the past year found a trapped moose that they liberated from
his pain by means of a pocketknife; that night they feasted
well. Sawyer's Rock was just past Sawyer's River, at the confluence of which the flow of the Saco changed to the east. As
light began to fade the travelers stopped at Emery's Tavern.
Belknap and Little joined Evans in staying for the night while
Cutler, Heard, Bartlett, Hubbard, Wingate, and Place pursued
the track another four miles to McMillan's. Enoch Emery's
tavern was at Bartlett, which marked the confluence of the
Rocky Branch and Saco rivers. The original proprietor of the
land was William Stark; the first settlers were Enoch and
Humphrey Emery. Enoch, who ran the tavern, was good-
natured and hospitable.

While enjoying Emery's hospitality, Belknap and Little did some figuring. They conceptualized the Great Range of mountains to be an "isosceles triangle," encompassing fifty square miles. They guessed there were at least ten mountain summits that they saw on their seventy-mile journey. "But it is impossible to tell the exact number," Belknap joked, "unless we should make an aerial voyage, in a balloon." Belknap, the student of the human and natural history of New England, was in awe that he himself had seen the region's "grand reservoir of waters." *"If the roads were clear on the back of the Mountains, you might in the same day drink of waters of Saco, Amariscogin, and Connecticut."* Belknap reveled in his new-found knowledge, which dispelled the ancient mysteries of the White Mountains.

The next morning, Thursday, July 29, Belknap, Little, and Evans rose early and set out for McMillan's to breakfast. There the nine men reunited briefly, before departing in different directions. While Belknap, Little, and Evans breakfasted, describing their adventures to the audience of tavern-goers, one Captain Heath disputed their claim to have climbed the highest mountain. Without adequate measurements, who can be certain? Belknap recalled Governor Wentworth and Nicholas Austin's uncertainty about which mountain was highest. The issue of the pond on the summit—accounts of its apparent existence fluctuating over the years according to different observers—continued to perplex Belknap. Doubt set into the scientific mind. Not so with Evans, who engaged in a lively dispute with Heath. If Heath (christened either Benjamin or Joshua) climbed any of the White Mountains, it is not recorded. But Evans had—twice. He *knew*, not logically but intuitively, and said as much. The debate, however, would continue.

After breakfast the two clergymen accompanied Captain Evans down the Saco to the great bend, when they, along with the river, turned sharply east. Before they departed Conway they encountered the same local women who, days before, requested that the ministers "lay the spirits" of the mountains.

Belknap and Little, offended that they were seen as "conjurers," refused to associate with the *vulgar* women. Evans, more their type, joked that indeed, the "invisible beings," among them Passaconaway, had been quieted. Perhaps Evans was right. Belknap, Cutler, Little, Fisher, and Whipple had penetrated the mountains, had discovered nothing so mysterious as to defy rational explanation, had measured and recorded, hypothesized and theorized. In time, the legends of thunder on a clear day, of carbuncles, of Passaconaway's curse would, like the mountain fog, dissipate in the wake of the spreading light of knowledge of the sublimity of God's work.

*Chapter Six*

# THE WEIGHT OF MORTALITY

D awn shed light on the verdure world tinged in the gray of early morning. Water dripped from fir trees; dense fog lay upon the pond; moisture imbued all things. Singing birds occasionally interrupted the quiet. The loon's call pierced the shrouded pond. Soon the tallest pines revealed the rising sun and basked in its light. The fog began to lift; still water, mirrorlike, emerged from slumber. Ripples here and there indicated to predators in flight where to look for prey. Sunlight slowly descended along the trunks of trees to the water. The wind picked up and curled the water forward in waves. Along the shore the sun's rays pierced the surface, disclosing the path of clams busy during the night. Sunfish darted about, feeding. The forest world, now fully awake and alive, was the same as yesterday, would be the same tomorrow. Then the men came.

Having dined at Porter's Tavern along the road to Fryeburg, and having arrived at Fryeburg after noon, Evans invited Belknap and Little to his farm at Lovewell's Pond. Belknap particularly wanted to see the infamous site of Lovewell's Battle. Evans piloted his two visitors along the route to the past, showing them the lay of the land, the marks of spent musketballs on trees, and the names of the dead carved into trunks. Evans related the vision and words of those who had once lived so long ago. His stories combined with Belknap's visual experience of the tour to give the historian a clear sense of what happened that day in 1725. Belknap felt ready to describe the incident in detail in the second volume of his *History of New-Hampshire*. The notes that he took in his handwritten journal served that purpose.

After the tour of the pond Belknap and Little met briefly with Major James Osgood, Evans' friend, who told the historian that he had helped survey the Maine/New Hampshire province line in 1768. The two ministers spent the night at the tavern of another local leader, Captain Henry Brown, before proceeding home the next morning. They left a town that still struggled to make ends meet on the fringes of civilization, a town hard pressed to build and maintain a meeting-house, good roads, and a school. The Fryeburg inhabitants, farmers, hunters, and traders, had limited personal wealth. John Evans thrived owning two oxen, four cattle, seven sheep, and three swine. Such success was tenuous in the northern frontier. The 1785 freshet that swelled the Saco and destroyed so much intervale farmland did not spare the Evans farm. Two years later Evans helped other town leaders instruct Moses Ames, the delegate to the ratifying convention held at Boston. Ames voted against adopting the Constitution, reflecting the beliefs of Evans, Frye, and others that the document gave Congress too much power and did not put enough emphasis on Christian sentiments. A few years later, hoping that Fryeburg would do its part to promote "Knowledge and Virtue," Evans served on a committee intent on erecting Fryeburg Academy. The young scholars of the academy sometimes went on excursions, even to the White Mountains. Perhaps John Evans led this new generation of thinkers to penetrate the wilderness of the northern forest.

Evans continued road-building beyond his sixtieth birthday. For years he served as surveyor of highways for the town, getting paid the standard five shillings for a day's work. But after 1792 Evans, a grandfather several times over, retired to his farm. The trails of the northern forest continued their annual call, particularly in the autumn. Evans answered the final call of the wilderness on May 17, 1807.

Belknap and Little departed Fryeburg "at half past six" the morning of July 30, 1784. Four hours riding along the Saco brought them to the "great falls," which "we judged not more than 40 feet perpendicular, though the descent may be as many rods." From the Saco they crossed overland to the Great Ossipee River, which, it lacking a bridge, they had to cross by means of a canoe that "an old woman paddled." The Little Ossipee River, twelve miles distance, fortunately had a bridge. They "lodged at Captain Smith's." The two men "parted" that Saturday morning, Little journeying to his home at Kennebunk, Belknap going to Dover. Along the way Belknap hired a guide to pilot him through a forest, baptized a newborn, visited a friend, and joined up with a hapless husband "whose wife had run away with . . . 25 of his dollars" and a "borrowed horse," for which he was responsible, to join the Shaker sect. The husband was "in pursuit" at least of the horse and money, if not his wife. Belknap, who did not have "*such* a wife," "got home well, about sunset."

Daniel Little likewise enjoyed his final day of travel, observing the "extraordinary" agricultural and structural "improvements" of Maine. Reaching the parsonage that evening he gave thanks that "through the care of heaven in this tour, man and beast have been suprizingly preserved from harm." Little, who was twenty years older than Belknap, maintained his energy and exuberance during the next two decades before his death in 1801, serving science, his parish, and the Society for Propagating the Gospel. He journeyed in 1785, 1786, and again in 1790 to the Penobscot region to instruct settlers and to cajole the natives to reject Catholicism for Protestantism—the Indians refused.

Manasseh Cutler, meanwhile, returned to his parish at Ipswich Village to carry on his many interests in botany, medicine, theology, and politics. Cutler, a graduate of Yale, was nevertheless much involved in Harvard College affairs. He sponsored several young scholars who sought admission to Harvard; one wonders whether or not Cutler sponsored Dudley Hubbard and John Bartlett as well. If nothing else, Cutler was perhaps instrumental in their participation in the journey to the wilderness. Evidence that the two boys thought of Cutler as their mentor grows when considering a paper, "A Description of the Ascent of the White Mountains in NH, explored by Bartlett and myself [Hubbard], Saturday, July 26th, 1784," apparently submitted as part of a course requirement to Harvard professor Samuel Gardner, who signed and "accepted" it. Ironically Gardner accepted a plagiarized paper: Hubbard and Bartlett's account is identical to Cutler's journal. Was it pure plagiarism, or just a test of penmanship?

As soon as Cutler was settled at the parsonage, he collected his journal notes and observations and tried to ascertain the height of the Great Mountain. Cutler's barometric and temperature readings led him to calculate the height at "10,000.1 feet above the level of the sea, and 6513.1 above our tent at the foot of the mountain. The tent 3488.5 feet above the level of the sea." On the Great Mountain, however, "air bubbles intruded into the tube," clearly affecting the result. Cutler hypothesized that his calculation was off by 20 percent, so guessed that the height was "9062.5 feet," but he was not sure; his uncertainty aggravated him. "It is . . . no small mortification to me not to be able to give a more accurate account of the height of this mountain, after taking so much pains to ascertain it." Even so, a nine-thousand-foot peak must place "the White Mountain . . . in no inconsiderable rank among the highest mountains on the globe," fifth only to the "Andes, 20,280; Peak of Teneriffe, 13,178; Gammi, 10,110; . . . and Mt. Blanc, 14,432."

During subsequent months the two scientists, Belknap and Cutler, corresponded about new observations and theories about the Great Mountain and plans to journey again thither to ascertain more accurate measurements. Joseph Haven of Rochester sent Belknap a descriptive log of changes in the mountain's appearance; it was not "uniformly white," clothed in snow, until November, which surprised Cutler. He thought the "unusual mildness of the atmosphere during the fall months explained the late snow." In January Cutler received from London his order of a "barometer and thermometer . . . made by Nairne & Blunt," which were "excellent instruments" but hardly "portable," which he needed for his next journey to the White Mountains. Belknap continued to send the latest about the mountain (and the mountaineers) from New Hampshire. George Place sent Belknap a sample of "copper ore" that Belknap forwarded to Cutler for inspection. Joseph Whipple's "sedate, observant, and critical eye," according to Belknap, "has been busy about the Mountains ever since, and he doubts" that the Great Mountain is highest. Captain Heath, it appears, got to him! Whipple "is suspicious that the highest peak is westward of that you ascended." Belknap, who acted unsure, should have recalled that Wentworth and Austin had settled that issue. Whipple's suspicions continued for years. By the time he put expression to his natural history interest in *The History of Acadie, Penobscot Bay and River* in 1816, he had accepted, even added to Belknap and Cutler's erroneous calculation of the Great Mountain's height, putting it at 11,000 feet. Even so, Whipple did not think that the Great Mountain was as high as Maine's Mt. Katahdin. Whipple wrote at length about the journey in 1805 of explorers to Maine's highest mountain; he recorded uncritically their guess, based on dream and supposition rather than science, that Katahdin's height was 13,000 feet—an overestimate of almost 8,000 feet.

Joseph Whipple also wrote to Belknap at large about "the freshet on the 4th of December," which "was the highest ever known in those parts." Whipple's farm at Dartmouth, like John Evans' at Fryeburg and Andrew McMillan's at Conway, were casualties of the freshet. "The new road at the [Western] Notch is greatly damaged." Belknap suspected that Evans' improvements to the Shelburne Road had similarly been destroyed: "That whole region must, from its nature, be subject to frequent changes by floods." Belknap also told Cutler about Daniel Little's recent visit to the Belknap parsonage. Little informed Ruth Belknap that the men of the journey "were all married for life." When Enoch Wingate visited a few days later "there was," Belknap supposed, "an air of familiarity and satisfaction in Wingate" that led Ruth to christen him "a White Hill man," although she had "never seen Wingate before."

The first journey was sufficiently successful that already

there was talk of a second. "The New River," Belknap wrote Cutler, "is by all"—Wingate, Little, Belknap, and Whipple—"pitched upon as the place where the next ascent ought to be made." Whipple thought that the next ascent "will not be practicable till about the 25th of June." Belknap agreed that June was best. "But my opinion is of no consequence. Two hundred-weight of mortality, and a pair of lungs by no means related to the *adamantine ones*, which [Alexander] Pope was laughed at so much about, are very inconvenient in the ascending line, unless an aerostatic machine could be contrived, and even then I suspect my brain would be giddy with the sudden elevation. It is a discouraging circumstance to my making a second attempt." Cutler responded in February 1785, "that June will be preferable to July, but I feel some discouragement about making the attempt at all. This cold snowy winter has considerably cooled my zeal, but when I get thawed out, in the spring, perhaps it may return." Ruth Belknap's "quick discovery of White Hill people, by their singular airs, has distorted my risibles and given my sides a hearty shake. Woods and mountains, it seems, may form people's manners, as well as assemblys and dancing-schools. What curious courtesies and compliments we should have, from a company of ladies, after a tour through those dreary regions!" Meanwhile Dr. Joshua Fisher informed Cutler that "he still feels the good effects of the shower-bath" he received north of the mountains and thinks "it may be best to repeat it next summer. He retains his White Mountain airs, and even our good friend Mr. Heard is strongly tinctured with them."

By the following April Cutler had regained his interest in a forthcoming return trip, partly because he felt that he owed it to the "Author of Nature" to explore nature, discover "natural productions," and generate a renewed interest in science. In June 1785 he wrote Belknap, "I feel anxious to make another attempt for measuring the White Mountains, but find so many difficulties in the way that I have given up the thought of going this year"—almost. One "Count Castiglioni, an Italian gentleman from Milan," interested in seeing the sights, expressed his interest in joining Cutler on a mountain excursion. Once the count returned from a journey to the Penobscot region of Maine, Cutler hoped to accompany him to the White Mountains.

Belknap, convinced it was foolish to attempt the Great Mountain again, was content to read and write about the White Mountains. Daniel Little sent him news about his recent journey to "the upper part of Penobscot River, in one notch of which is a mountain, which the Indians call Tadden, *i.e.*, the highest [Katahdin], and say it is bald-pated like our Saconian [White] Mountains, and exceeds them in altitude." The Maine Indians told John Gyles the same thing sixty to seventy years earlier. "Asking their pardon," Belknap responded, "I think them very poor judges, as it is well known they have no mode of mensuration, and are afraid to ascend high mountains, lest they should invade the Territory of *Hobomocko*," the Devil. During his journey to Philadelphia in 1785, Belknap spoke with David Rittenhouse, who informed the scientist that the Allegheny Mountains are steep on the east side, with a gradual slope on the west. Belknap agreed "that the Eastern sides of *all* mountains are steepest, owing to the descent of the waters of the deluge," the Great Flood.

Belknap wrote about the journey to the White Mountains in volume three of the *History of New-Hampshire*, and he provided a long treatise for the *Transactions* of the American Philosophical Society. Upon returning from the journey in August 1784, he dashed off several letters to family and friends, telling his young son Samuel that "eight of our Company went to the top and were seven hours getting there. I went up for two hours but my breath failed and I was obliged to return. They are exceeding steep." "We went all round the Mountains and lodged in the woods three nights." "The Cause of their whiteness is the snow and ice which commonly lies on them nine or ten months in the year." "We saw the heads of several large Rivers which rise in those Mountains, the water runs very quick and with great descent. There are some streams which afford a most beautiful prospect, falling down from steep rocks, or winding along their crooked channels, or spreading on the flat surface of them. Had you been there and had time you might have caught plenty of Trouts."

Belknap reserved his most detailed comments for his friend Ebenezer Hazard. Belknap continued to feel the effects of the journey to the Great Mountain even a week after his return to Dover. Disappointment that he failed to reach the summit still lingered. Having felt to a high degree the weight of mortality, Belknap confessed to his friend that "I have not such an opinion of long life in this world as some people are fond of entertaining." Yet he was more aware than ever of the "comfort" of "Heaven," "the promise of salvation," "a patient resignation to the divine will, and an increase of love to the divine character and ways."

Having promised Hazard a detailed narrative, Belknap set to it on Tuesday, August 16. This brand of history based on personal observation was especially popular among eighteenth-century literati, and Belknap delighted in it. "It was on Friday morning, the 23d of July, that we set off from Conway, and took our leave of *house and bed* for 3 days, to make a genuine tour in the wilderness." John Evans, "our pilot," following in the wake of Darby Field, Richard Vines, and John Josselyn, "judged it best for us to go up a branch of Saco River to the *height of land* between that and Amariscogin waters; then we could ascend the Mountain by *a ridge which is one continued ascent* to the top. Had we attempted it in any other part," as had, perhaps, Neal, as well as Wells, Wentworth, and Austin, "*we must have ascended and descended several mountains before we could have reached the summit*." "Saturday, July 24, at 6 1/4 A.M., we began our ascent" of the Great Mountain. The portly Belknap had no need to tell his friend that "I was not the nimblest, and the pauses were the more frequent on my account." After his return to camp, Belknap and Fisher waited it out until morning, when the mountaineers arrived and told them of the plain and the Sugar Loaf. "The next morning, i.e., Sunday, 25, after breakfast, we set off for Mr. Whipple's plantation, which was the nearest

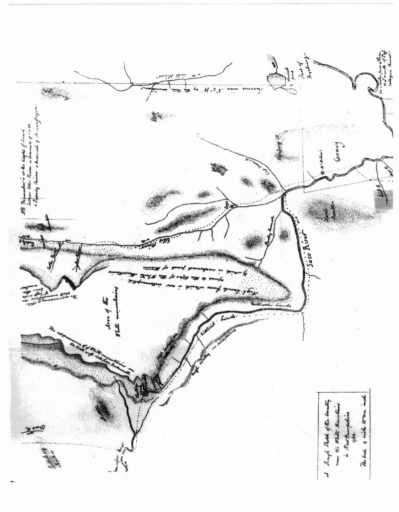

*A Rough Sketch of the Country Near the White Mountains.* Jeremy Belknap's sketch, which he appended to a letter to Ebenezer Hazard, includes the route taken during the July 1784 journey as well as an illustrative description of the principal rivers of the region and several panoramic views of the mountains. *Dartmouth College Library.*

*human* habitation on the way we wished to go." During the rainy night on the path to Whipple's in which the men bivouacked in the forest, Belknap "could not help calling to mind" Laurence Sterne's *The Life and Opinions of Tristram Shandy, Gentleman,* in which he describes "the situation of poor Uncle Toby and Corporal Trim, at the siege of Limerick, when the *radical moisture* prevailed over the *radical heat,* and they supplied the latter by burnt brandy." The next morning they "got through these dismal *roads,* and arrived at Mr. Whipple's plantation." Belknap concluded the letter noting that "the foregoing has been written piecemeal. . . . I have not time to finish it; so you must excuse the rest till another week."

Three days later, pen in hand, Belknap continued the story. He hastened to reassure Hazard that "I did . . . earnestly wish for your company" on the trip. At Whipple's "it was our design to have made a geometrical measuration of the height of the Mountains" but for the ubiquitous clouds. Belknap, instead, "took a sketch of them," a copy of which he enclosed for his friend's benefit. "Wednesday, July 28. At 6h., morning, we took our leave of this place, set out southward on our return." At the Western Notch Belknap gazed upon "a most *sublimely* picturesque and romantic scene!" The notch was the quickest route from the seacoast to the Upper Cohos; as Hazard was Postmaster General of the United States, Belknap discussed the advisability of establishing a post office nearby. Upon departing the notch, the men came to "the Flume," one of "two beautiful cascades" that tumble down the west side of the Great Mountain. "These beauties of Nature gave me inexpressible delight." Descending the Saco to Conway Belknap spied, "on the sides of these mountains, at immense heights, and in places perfectly inaccessible, . . . rocks, some of whitish and some of a reddish hue, their sides polished by the continual trickling of water over them. These, when incrusted with ice, being open toward the S. and W., reflect the moon and starbeams in the night, and are sufficient to give rise to the fiction of *carbuncles,* which the Indians and their captives used to report, and which have swelled into marvellous and incredible stories among the vulgar." "I have been asked, since I came home, whether I did not hear *terrible noises* among the mountains. O the power of nonsense, superstition, and folly! When will mankind make use of their senses and be wise!" "Thursday, July 29, I parted with most of the company, who were returning by the way we came, while I had a mind to go down Saco River, in company with Mr. Little." "Saturday P.M. arrived safe at home." Cutler since then had written Belknap of his estimates of mountain heights. Belknap reported to Hazard that "the appearances in these mountainous regions are extremely deceptive, and it will take a person several days to get used to them, so as to know how to form any tolerable judgment of heights and distances." Belknap continued: "I have now, my dear sir, given you an account of what I *have* seen. . . . To complete my narrative, however, I must tell you what I have *not* seen": "no *silver mines*," nor lead, no "*limestone*, which would have been of more service to the country than silver or gold mines," nor rattlesnakes, "nor hobgoblins, demons, nor cacodemons, no wandering ghosts, nor the least appearance of *Hobamoke*, though I suppose Dr. [Cotton] Mather would have said we had invaded his territories, being 'Prince of the Power of the *Air*'!" "Should you ask what is the cause of the *white* appearances of these Mountains, I would tell you in one word,—*snow*, which lies on them, commonly, from September or October till July." Belknap concluded his letter jesting: "From the account given in these letters of the White Mountains, you will be able to correct one which . . . I formerly sent you a copy of written by G[eneral John] S[ullivan] to Marbois, and you will see an essential difference between a first and second-hand description in point of propriety,—I mean not of rhetorical flourish."

Belknap never again experienced adventure to match the White Mountains—although on a few occasions he came close. In 1785 he visited Philadelphia not as an explorer but as a father visiting a son (Joseph) and a scientist drawn to the center of science in the new nation. Two years later Belknap relocated to Boston to take another church; this move and new clerical duties restricted his travel but not his scholarly pursuit of knowledge about the White Mountains and early American explorers. In 1792 he published volume three of the *History of New-Hampshire*, a complete natural history of the state. Two years later he published a collective biography of European explorers of America, the *American Biography*. In 1796 Belknap joined geographer Jedidiah Morse in a natural history and missionary journey to upstate New York. The following year Belknap and Noah Webster sailed in search of the lost Gosnold colony—they found it on Cuttyhunk Island, south of Massachusetts.

Belknap had been dead six years, and Daniel Little three, when sixty-two-year-old Manasseh Cutler fulfilled his dream of once again journeying to and ascending the Great Mountain. Cutler had since 1785 experienced many false alarms respecting his intended journey. Count Castiglioni never showed up the summer of 1785. Two years later, in 1787, Cutler intended "to ascend" the "White Mountain, which is undoubtedly the highest in any of the United States," accompanied by "Samuel Vaughan, of Philadelphia." Cutler and Vaughan hoped to imitate Sir George Shuckburgh's successful measurement of two peaks in the Alps in 1775 and 1776. But it was not to be in 1787.

Finally, in July 1804, Cutler succeeded. Accompanying Cutler were friends such as Jonathan Dodge and Harvard professors such as William Dandridge Peck and Samuel Gardner. Cutler was amply "prepared" with "instruments" to determine the mountain's height. His servant, Jesse, accompanied him to Dudley Tyng's home at Newburyport, where Cutler rendezvoused with six of his colleagues. From here to Wells Tavern at Hampton Falls, the men traveled by chaise and a "coach and four." Belknap having departed Dover twenty years before, his family now in Boston, the men "lodged at Gage's" tavern at Dover. Joseph Haven, still examining the Great Mountain by light of day, fed them breakfast at his Rochester parsonage. Following the same path as in 1784, they journeyed to Ossipee River and Pond, where they "botanized on the shore." One phenomenon had not changed in twenty years: the "road excessively bad." The next day they stopped for a meal at McMillan's Tavern, still run by the family, though the old Irishman had died a few years before. After a brief stop the men proceeded along the Saco to Emery's Tavern at Bartlett, where they spent the night. The next morning they prepared for the ascent. The plan this time was quite different from before. The men journeyed up the Ellis on the old Shelburne Road but "found the road so obstructed with trees, [we were] obliged to send our horses back." They "proceeded on foot to New River and the Meadow, in the East Notch." They ascended through the trees along New River and made camp for the night in the mountain forest. Cutler reported that he "slept very well" in "a sort of tent, covered with boughs."

The morning of the ascent, the scientists "placed a barometer and thermometer in the shade." Five pilots led the seven scientists. They reached the *krummholz* after "two hours" traveling. "We were obliged to get on the tops of the trees, which became shorter and shorter, although the trunks were large and the tops spreading, having been pressed down with an almost perpetual body of snow." As they pursued the ascent above tree line, extreme fatigue forced two guides and three scientists to halt and descend to camp. The others continued on an incline that Cutler thought "was elevated 60° from a horizontal line." Upon reaching the plain, "we had a view of about nine ascending summits, which rose to different heights from broad rocky bases, and seemed very much to limit the vegetation of mosses, grasses, and low shrubs." The vegetation that did exist "gave the rocks a spotted appearance of different colors, whitish, reddish, brownish, and rusty." They ascended several ridges, then the Sugar Loaf, "which is the highest part of the mountain." On the summit Cutler was preoccupied with setting up his barometer and thermometer and measuring the levels of mercury. He used a theodolite to guarantee that the Great Mountain was indeed the highest. It was a hazy, yet sunny day, and sufficiently cool on the summit that when

they "began our descent" Cutler was "very much chilled."
Snow still lay on the side of the mountain—in July! "Our fatigue in descending was extreme." The air nevertheless "in-
vigorated" them; finding a spring to quench their thirst was
an inexpressible delight. "We entered the wood in a deep valley to the southward of our ascent, where we made a fire, at
dark, and slept without any tent or cover." The next morning
they returned to camp—eventually. The guides led them in
the spirit of John Evans, by a gut feeling rather than actual
knowledge or maps. Of course they got lost. The impatient
and frustrated scientists waited and rested and were "obliged
to send our guides back to find" the camp "and bring our baggage" hither.

The need for such guides waned with each passing year.
True, Abel Crawford and his son Ethan guided visitors to the
summit for many years. This was hardly necessary after 1861,
with the completion of the carriage road up the Great Mountain to the summit. At mid-century the White Mountains
were less the province of the hunter, wilderness guide, and
intrepid scientist and more a tourist attraction. The subsequent few decades after Cutler's ascent of 1804 were transi-
tional years of visits by an increasing number of scientists
such as Jacob Bigelow, theologians such as Timothy Dwight,
philosophers such as Henry David Thoreau, and artists such
as Abel Bowen. The engraver Bowen in 1816 produced a romantic print of the majestic Western Notch just as Jeremy
Belknap envisioned it: a sublime and grand portrait of a benevolent Creation.

The same year, 1816, Dr. Jacob Bigelow, "Lecturer on Materia Medica and Botany, in Harvard University," explored the
White Mountains and wrote a clear journalistic and scientific
account of his journey. Bigelow was able to correct some errors
of past knowledge. He knew, for example, that European
mountains dwarfed their New England counterparts. He was
unsure, however, whether or not the White Mountains were
the highest in America—at least they were in the United

*Abel Bowen engraving,* The Gap of the White Mountains, *1816. Abel Bowen's engraving, produced in the same year that Dr. Jacob Bigelow journeyed to Mount Washington, captures the sublime and romantic qualities with which his contemporaries viewed the Western (Crawford) Notch of the White Mountains.* New Hampshire Historical Society.

States of his day, he thought, and perhaps even in the Louisiana Territory. He assumed, but was not entirely convinced, that Darby Field was the first to ascend the White Mountains.

Bigelow journeyed in July 1816, approaching the mountains from the northwest, rather like Captain Wells. Bigelow, however, passed through the Western Notch and followed the road paralleling the Saco to its confluence with the Ellis River. He ascended the Ellis until he arrived at Cutler's River, which became the route of ascent. Bigelow clearly agreed with Captain Evans' choice of Cutler's River as "leading directly to the summit." Bigelow continued to refer to the mountain's three zones, echoing Cutler. He climbed "the primary peak, the one designated in Winthrop's Journal, by the name of *sugar loaf.*" He agreed with John Josselyn that the summit affords a view of the surrounding country that "is daunting terrible." Bigelow like Belknap and Cutler sought to determine the height of the highest summit. He knew Cutler's calculations from his 1784 and 1804 journeys; his own team of scientists arrived at the reasonable figure of 6,225 feet. He agreed with Belknap's conclusion that the mountains are white simply because of the snow. Bigelow fulfilled Cutler's dream of compiling a complete list, based on the Linnaean system, of the flora, especially the alpine variety, of the White Mountains. In light of Bigelow's account, one sees clearly that by 1816 scientific New England had arrived at logical, empirical solutions for the many mysteries of Passaconaway's realm.

# "Mount Washington"

George Washington never journeyed to the White Mountains of central New Hampshire. Yet in the years after the Belknap/Cutler expedition of 1784, New Englanders honored Washington by naming the highest and grandest peak of New England "Mount Washington." For centuries the mountain had been called native and nondescript names: Agiocochook, the "Chrystall Hill," the "twinkling mountain," the White Hill, the Great White Mountain, the Mountain, the Great Mountain. Such names referred to a distant, mysterious peak. But after 1784 the Great Mountain seemed no longer distant and not so mysterious; rather it was a monument to the wilderness conquered and made known by American civilization. The recognized leader of this civilization was George Washington.

General Washington was a hero to Jeremy Belknap as he was to many, especially conservative, Americans. Belknap wrote Hazard in April 1783 at the conclusion of the War for Independence that Washington was "that illustrious chief whom Providence raised up and supported to add a peculiar dignity to the noble struggle in which America has been obliged to engage in support of her rights and liberties.... How happy to be born and live in an age which has produced so excellent a man!" While Belknap journeyed to the White Mountains a letter accompanying his first volume of the *History of New-Hampshire* was on its way to Mount Vernon. Belknap asked General Washington to accept "the first Volume of a work in which you will see the early struggles and Sufferings of one of those States which claims the honor of being defended by your sword; and which though in the late arduous Conflict it has not been so much exposed as in former

Wars yet having long been a nursery of stern heroism has bred an hardy race of men whose merits as soldiers are well known to their beloved General and who will always glory in having assisted to plant the Laurel which adorns his brow."

It was Belknap's third volume of the *History of New-Hampshire* that christened, at least for the literary and scientific world, the Great Mountain as Mount Washington: "The mountain which makes so majestic an appearance all along the shore . . . has lately been distinguished by the name of *Mount WASHINGTON."* These merging circumstances—that Belknap's description of his 1784 journey to the White Mountains coincides in the book with the use of Mount Washington for the first time, as well as Belknap's particular veneration for the general—do not yield the standard and accepted conclusion among authors that Belknap, Cutler, Evans, and the others christened Mount Washington during their 1784 journey. Indeed they did not, as the year-long correspondence of Jeremy Belknap and Manasseh Cutler, in which they refer to "the White Mountain" and "the Mountain," but not to "Mount Washington," illustrates conclusively. Cutler, as late as October 1786, was still referring to the "White Mountain." The perfect occasion to christen the mountain would have been Belknap's report to the American Philosophical Society, in which he referred to it as "the highest summit," "the sugarloaf," and "the mountain."

Nevertheless Jeremy Belknap was more instrumental than any of his contemporaries in associating the Great Mountain with General Washington. Belknap's letters to Ebenezer Hazard and other American scientists, his report to the American Philosophical Society published in their *Transactions* and reprinted in 1788 in the *American Museum*, as well as volumes one and two of the *History of New-Hampshire*, made the White Mountains in general and the Great Mountain in particular well known. Then the new president of the United States, George Washington, decided to take a trip.

Washington determined after taking office in 1789 "to acquire knowledge of the face of the Country, the growth and Agriculture thereof—and the temper and disposition of the Inhabitants toward the new government." He set out from New York on October 15, 1789, and arrived in Boston ten days later. Belknap, part of the lengthy entourage awaiting the president, had written Hazard a few days before that "a family of children cannot receive a long absent parent with more real joy than will be felt by the citizens of this place on his coming." Washington arrived in New Hampshire the last day of October and stopped at Wells' Tavern, where he spoke with veterans of the Revolution. "At his entrance" to Portsmouth, the *New Hampshire Gazette* reported, "he was saluted by thirteen cannon from three companies of Artillery.... The street through which he passed (Congress Street) was lined by the citizens of the town, all the crafts[men] being arranged alphabetically; the Bells rang a joyful peal, and repeated shouts from grateful thousands, hail'd their Deliverer welcome to the Metropolis of New-Hampshire."

> Behold he comes! Columbia's pride,
> And Nature's boast—her fav'rite Son,
> Of valour—wisdom—truth—well try'd—
> Hail, matchless WASHINGTON.

To the New Englanders of the time Washington was a savior, flesh and blood to be sure but set apart all the same, chosen by providence to lead America from bondage to freedom. He was a hero like those of the past—Moses, Pericles, Scipio; a man of bravery, resolution, piety, self-sacrifice, and patience. He never gave up on the cause and saw it all the way through. No Caesar or Cromwell, he supported the republic best by laying aside his sword, as did Cincinnatus for Rome. The first president of a government of order, he was himself controlled in his words, bearing, and actions. Already Washington was becoming a monument, an icon of myth and legend elevated beyond himself, the plains and valleys of a normal man. The Reverend Joseph Buckminster of Portsmouth's First Parish embarrassed himself as well as the general in his address of Sunday, November 1:

We see the Man whom heaven designed as the principal instrument of accomplishing one of the greatest revolutions in the nations of the

*Sunset at the White Mountains.* With the close of the eighteenth century the sun set on an image of the White Mountains and the Great Mountain as a "daunting terrible" region isolated from the familiarity of civilized society and modern science. *Dartmouth College Library.*

earth. . . . We see the MAN endued . . . with that rare assemblage of qualities which unites the jarring interests, views and affections of an extensive continent. . . . We see the GENERAL, who, with a cool, intrepid bravery, faced every danger; with unexampled firmness sustained every discouragement; and, with persevering magnanimity, surmounted every obstacle. . . . We now see this illustrious PATRIOT, like the father of a great family, visiting the various branches, to bless and to be blessed, to start the tear of joy and awaken mutual congratulations.

Such extravagance continued for days. Washington was toasted at parties, painted by artists, hailed by dignitaries, serenaded and almost worshipped until he was forced, no doubt for sanity's sake, to leave Portsmouth "quietly, and without any attendance." After his departure the inhabitants, at a loss who to laud, celebrate, and idolize, searched, one imagines, for a visible counterpart, something solid and immovable like the general, resolute and imposing, towering above all others in utter force, even violence, yet bringing peace, order, constancy, sameness, an image of unstoppable power, unbridgeable force. Who else to name the Great Mountain after than *Washington?*

It was of course necessary to name the mountain soon after the Belknap/Cutler journey into the wilderness. It is the way of science, of civilization, to analyze, arrange, order, possess, control, and name that which is hitherto unknown, uncontrolled, random, savage, wild, unnamed. *Agiocochook* had to become something else. So, too, did *White Hill* and *Great Mountain*, names that indicated something only vaguely known, incompletely understood, distant and impenetrable. If Belknap and Cutler did not christen Mount Washington, he who did had the same scientific, urbane, rational, civilized assumptions. Perhaps John Evans joined ranks as well and referred to the Great Mountain as Mount Washington. If he did, it was slightly out of character for the man who found the Great Mountain mirrored in himself: a thing felt and not completely known, sensed but rarely seen, with a hidden force and majesty, silently dignified, touched by heaven in a way few can know, christened not by name but by spirit, a distant rugged peak, a daunting wilderness.

# Appendix

*A Description of the ascent of the White Mountains in NH explor'd by Bartlet & myself, Saturday July 26th, 1784.*

We set off from our camp 6 minutes after 6, clock AM. The ascent was in general pretty uniform from the tent, the growth below very tall consisting of spruce, hemlock & pine, I suppose more than 100 feet, our ascent I suppose 25 to 45 [degrees] varying in places from one to the other. We ascended on the North side of a river which run down from the Mt. but crossing it to the S. some ways below the clear. The stones in this river were curious, containing talc, starry appearances & many were very light. We ascended the Mt. after we had crossed the river until the growth, which gradually diminished, became low shrubs having cross'd the growth of various kinds of wood in our way. In passing through the shrubs which were from 10 to 2 feet in height, we were greatly fatigued sometimes crawling under them, at others we mounted on to their tops, & were frequently supported by them for several steps until we plung'd thro them, our guides often wishing for their snow-shoes, & I thought with very good reason, with which they imagined that they could walk very well on their tops. But this time of walking did not extend above 60 or 70 rods before we came into what is call'd the clear, which [is] above the trees, & is judg'd to be about two thirds the way up the Mt. The Mt. above the shrubs has the appearance of a close fed pasture with many detach'd rocks rising from the surface, as we advanc'd we found it to be a mat of long mosses, their crevices fill'd up with various kinds of vegetables, most of them such as we had not seen before. Here we found a very short kind of vine which bare a fruit resembling the crane-berry, which were nearly quite ripe, those that were ripe were black, some of which I ate the taste very insipid. There are some other berries on stems about 2 or 3 inches high, & several vegetables in flower, there were large beds of what they call Laberdore Tea, of a very aromatic taste & smell. The Rev'd Mr. Cutler who was one of our company found near a spring what is call'd the Narcassus in bloom but the leaves were oblong, the smell agreeable; among the rocks were spruces about 3 or 4 inches high, which had been perhaps growing several 1000 years to obtain this height. The winds & snow had kept their tops even with the surface of the rocks, which made them appear as tho, they had been mow'd frequently, sufficiently firm to support us as we walk upon them; Near the border of the shrubs the declivity of the Mt. is not so steep as below, which is call'd the plain, tho, the ascent may be 15° or 20°. Our ascent after we pass'd over this plain was not less than 45 or 50 [degrees] until we reach'd the first summit. In many places the rocks are bare for a considerable distance in the course we ascended for several feet in width, & we greatly facilitated our ascent by climbing up those rocks which were large & detach'd; those long stripes of long bare rocks I presume gave rise to the notion of staircases, but they are without the least appearance of regularity, & were evidently washed bare by the descent of large torrents of waters occasion'd by the desolving of snow. While we were ascending this part of the Mt. a curious scene open'd to our view. Clouds were forming, moving & disipating by turns in every direction. For most of the time we had clear sunshine but repeatedly involved in clouds rolling on the sides of the Mt. The whole process of cloud making was apparent, & struck us with an agreable surprise, large columns arising from below, & ascending on each hand in the dark channels that were made by the descent of water, until they reach'd a colder & rarer region of the air, when they spread horizontally, & descended to these regions below. Towards the neighbouring mountains they appear in a different form as the clouds accumulate vapor from the vallies beneath, condensing in one part, dissipating in another, some columns rising, others falling, others moving in various directions; thus the regions of the atmosphere for many 1000 feet occupied by these vapors appear'd in the most delightful confusion, all in motion, & every direction at the same instant. When we were near the summit we were highly amused with large & dense clouds moving along the mountain perhaps a 1000 feet below us. As we ascended the first summit we had certainly one of the most extensive prospect that any part of N. America exhibits. This most mountainous part of the country was sunk into a plain as far as the sight of the eye cou'd reach, interspers'd with considerable moles to vary the prospect. It suggested the idea of viewing an extensive marsh from an iminece far above it, with numerous staks of hay settled down, & extending a broad base. Tho' the day was unfavorable for distant prospects, yet we saw the sea for a considerable distance from the summit. N.E.N. & N.W.—in these directions the plain was not so level, several mountains towred their heads, & seem'd to vie with those we were ascending, but still were far below them, & our view exceeding extensive. Our view to W. & S.W. was somewhat similar, the immense plain which the eye now commanded was of a beautiful verdure, variagated with the different shades of green, from the different trees that overspread it, & still diversify'd with a few settled plantations. When we had reach'd the first summit, we had arriv'd above the limits of vegetation. This summit is an irregular pinnacle of detach'd rocks of a dark grey colour, & seem'd to be compos'd of talk, flint, & hard grey stone. West & N.W. from this summit is an extensive plain with an easy declivity to the N.W. It appears like a smooth grass plot and maybe ¾ of a mile in extent. It was spread over with much the same kind of vegatables we had seen below the summit. In the S.W. part of this plain is the sugar loaf (as it is call'd) is situated. This also is an immense pile of detach'd rocks with the same kind of pinnacle, the ascent not so steep, as in some part of the mountains we had ascended, at the foot of it vegetation ceases. We were an hour & 21 minutes walking from the first summit to the pinnacle of the sugar loaf, & had the best walking of any part of our journey from the bottom of the Mt. Arriv'd at the pinnacle 6 minutes past one. Soon after we arriv'd, & before we had time to make any of those observations & measurements respecting distant objects for which purpose we had been at the trouble of carrying instruments to this height in the atmosphere, we had the misfortune to be involv'd in a dense cloud, with hope however that it would pass over as other clouds had done in our ascent. The sugarloaf was suppos'd by the company in general to be about 500 feet above the plain, we found on the heights of the rock an old hat which [was] left there in June 1774[;] one of our guides was of the party that left it. The cloud that involv'd us instead of dissipating and passing off as we hoped, increas'd in density until no object could be seen a very small distance, & was so dark as to appear like the near approach of night, we employ'd our selves in ingraving the first letters of our names in the rocks.

Bartlett
& Hubbard

# Essay on Sources

Manuscript sources upon which I based the narrative include materials found at the Massachusetts Historical Society (used by permission): Jeremy Belknap's "Several Accounts of the White Mountains," which is appended to his manuscript journal, "Journey to Dartmouth"; Daniel Little to Jeremy Belknap, September 8, 1766; Daniel Little to Jeremy Belknap, June 1784; Joseph Whipple to Jeremy Belknap, December 9, 1791; Jeremy Belknap to George Washington, July 19, 1784; "Acct of the White Mos. As Told by Mr Fesenden to Mr Haven"; and Dudley Hubbard and John Bartlett, "Description of the Ascent of the White Mountain in N.H., Explor'd by Bartlet & Myself Saturday July 26th, 1784." Materials used by permission at the New Hampshire Historical Society include Jeremy Belknap to Paine Wingate, January 20, 1785 and Jeremy Belknap to Samuel Belknap, September 2, 1784. Also used by permission is Daniel Little, "Tour of the White Mountains" (Typescript, Collection of the Brick Store Museum, Kennebunk, Maine).

Daniel Little's account is one of several descriptions of the Belknap/Cutler expedition of 1784. The most important are Jeremy Belknap, "Tour of the White Mountains," and Jeremy Belknap to Ebenezer Hazard, August 16 and 19, 1784, *Collections of the Massachusetts Historical Society*, series 5, vols. 2 and 3 (Boston: Massachusetts Historical Society, 1882, 1887). William P. and Julia P. Cutler, eds., *Life, Journals, and Correspondence of Rev. Manasseh Cutler, LL.D.*, 2 vols. (Cincinnati: Robert Clarke & Co., 1888), includes Cutler's unfinished account of the journey, along with many follow-up letters describing his discoveries. See also Belknap's account of the journey in the *Transactions of the American Philosophical So-*

*ciety*, vol. 2 (Philadelphia: Robert Aitken, 1786) and in the *American Museum*, vol. 3 (Philadelphia: Carey, 1788).

Belknap's manuscript "Several Accounts of the White Mountains" is the best single source of the history of White Mountain exploration, which one may supplement with his *The History of New Hampshire*, 3 vols. (Philadelphia and Boston: Robert Aitken, Thomas and Andrews, Belknap and Young, 1784, 1791, 1792), particularly volume three. For early ascents see James K. Hosmer, ed., *Winthrop's Journal: "History of New England," 1630–1649*, 2 vols. (New York: Charles Scribner's Sons, 1908). William Hubbard, in his *General History of New England—Collections of the Massachusetts Historical Society*, series 2, vols. 5 and 6 (Boston: Massachusetts Historical Society, 1816; reprint ed., New York: Johnson Reprint Corp, 1968)—combined into one anachronistic account Winthrop's three accounts of the two Darby Field journeys and the Gorges/Vines journey. For John Josselyn's journey see his *New-Englands Rarities Discovered* (London: G. Widdowes, 1672) and Paul Lindholdt, ed., *John Josselyn, Colonial Traveler: A Critical Edition of Two Voyages to New-England* (Hanover: University Press of New England, 1988). Other early narrative accounts are Charles E. Fay, ed., "The March of Captain Samuel Willard," *Appalachia* vol. 2; John Gyles, *Memoirs of the Odd Adventures, Strange Deliverances &c. In the Captivity of John Giles* . . . (Boston: Kneeland & Green, 1736); Robert Rogers, *A Concise Account of North America* (London: J. Millan, 1765); Jacob Bigelow, "Some Account of the White Mountains of New Hampshire," *The New England Journal of Medicine and Surgery* 5 (January 1816); Samuel Penhallow, *The History of the Wars of New-England with the Eastern Indians* (Boston: T. Fleet, 1726); Rev. Paul Coffin, "Ride to Piggwacket," in *Collections of the Maine Historical Society*, vol. 4, (Portland: MHS, 1856); Jacob B. Moore, "Historical Sketch of Concord, in the county of Merrimack, N.H.," in *Collections of the New-Hampshire Historical Society*, vol. 1, (Concord: Jacob Moore, 1824). Modern sources are Laura and Guy Waterman, *Forest and Crag: A History of Hiking, Trail Blazing, and Adventure in the Northeast Mountains* (Boston: Appalachian Mountain Club, 1989); Frederick Tuckerman, "Early Visits to the White Mountains and Ascents of the Great Range," *Appalachia* vol. 15; Warren W. Hart, "The First Ascent of the White Hill," *Appalachia* vol. 24; Frederick W. Kilbourne, *Chronicles of the White Mountains* (Boston: Houghton Mifflin Co., 1916); Allen H. Bent, "Early American Mountaineers," *Appalachia*, vol. 13: Bent describes the early Spanish-American ascents. For Conrad Gesner, see Charles E. Raven, *Natural Religion and Christian Theology*, vol. 1 (Cambridge: Cambridge University Press, 1953), chapter five.

I based much of *Passaconaway's Realm* on legends and antiquarian accounts. For stories of Passaconaway see Charles E. Beals, *Passaconaway in the White Mountains* (Boston: Richard G. Badger, 1916) and J. S. English, *Indian Legends of the White Mountains* (Boston: Rand Avery Supply Co., 1915). For stories of the White Mountains and the towns of the Saco Valley see George Hill Evans, *Pigwacket. Part 1: Old Indian Days in the Valley of the Saco* (Conway: New Hampshire Historical Society, 1939); Benjamin G. Willey, *Incidents in White Mountain History* (Boston: Noyes, 1856); Georgia Merrill, *History of Coos County* (Syracuse: W. A. Fergusson and Co., 1888); Benjamin Eastman, *North Conway: Its Surroundings, Its Settlement by English People* (North Conway: Reporter Press, n. d.).

I relied heavily on Belknap's *History of New-Hampshire* to re-create the life and times of John Evans. Evans' life however, is not well documented. Anecdotal information comes from John Stuart Barrows, *Fryeburg, Maine: An Historical Sketch* (Fryeburg: Pequawket Press, 1938); H. E. Mitchell, *The Town Register* (Brunswick, Maine: H. E. Mitchell Co., 1907); William Gordon, *History of Fryeburg* (Norway, Maine: G. W. Libby, 1933); G. T. Ridlon, *Saco Valley Settlements and Families* (Rutland, Vermont: Charles E. Tuttle Co., 1969); and Nathaniel Bouton, *The History of Concord*, (Concord: B. W. Sanborn, 1856). Additional data can be found in volumes one and two of the Fryeburg Town Records, Fryeburg Historical Society. The *First Census of the United States*, 1790, provides important information. Donna-Belle Garvin and James L. Garvin, *On the Road North of Boston: New Hampshire Taverns and Turnpikes, 1700–1900* (Concord: New Hampshire Historical Society, 1988) and Sarah S. Hughes, *Surveyors and Statesmen: Land Measuring in Colonial Virginia* (Richmond: Virginia Association of Surveyors, 1979), helped me understand Evans' road building techniques.

The lives and times of Evans' friends and associates are described in "Diaries of the Rev. Timothy Walker," *Collections of the New Hampshire Historical Society*, vol. 9 (Concord: Ira Evans, 1889); Caleb Stark, ed., *Memoir and Official Correspondence of Gen. John Stark* (Boston: Gregg Press, 1972); H. M. Jackson, *Rogers' Rangers: A History* (Aylmer East, Quebec: 1953); Warren W. Hart, "Timothy Nash," *Appalachia*, vol. 14; and Franklin McDuffee, *History of Rochester*, vol. 1 (Manchester: J. B. Clarke, 1897). Information about Daniel Little comes from Clifford Shipton, *Biographical Sketches of Those Who Attended Harvard College*, 14 vols. (Boston: Massachusetts Historical Society, 1933–1975), vol. 12. For Belknap's life and thought see Russell M. Lawson, *The American Plutarch: Jeremy Belknap and the Historian's Dialogue with the Past* (Westport: Praeger Publishers, 1998). For Joseph Whipple see Chester B. Jordan, *Colonel Joseph B. Whipple* (Concord: Republican Press Association, 1894); George Evans, *History of the Town of Jefferson, New Hampshire, 1773–1927* (Manchester: Granite State Press, 1927); Levi W. Dodge, "Colonel Joseph Whipple and His Dartmouth Plantation," *Granite Monthly* (January 1893); and Joseph Whipple, *The History of Acadie, Penobscot Bay and River* (Bangor, Maine: Peter Edes, 1816). For Joshua Fisher see Shipton, *Biographical Sketches*, vol. 16. Good general sources are Charles E. Clark, *The Eastern Frontier: The Settlement of Northern New England, 1610–1763* (Hanover: University Press of New England, 1983); Jere R. Daniell, *Colonial New Hampshire: A History* (Millwood, New York: KTO Press, 1981); F. Allen Burt, *The Story of Mount Washington* (Hanover: Dartmouth Publications, 1960).

Sources used to re-create the history of early perceptions of and journeys to the White Mountains include John Smith, "The Description of New England," in *The Complete Works of Captain John Smith*, ed. Philip Barbour, vol. 2 (Chapel Hill: University of North Carolina Press, 1986); Thomas Gorges, *America Painted to the Life* (London: N. Brook, 1658); John Ogilby, *America: Being the Latest, and Most Accurate Description of the New World . . .* (London: Author, 1671); Nathaniel Bouton, ed., *Documents and Records Relating to the Province of New-Hampshire*, vol. 1 (Concord: George Jenks, 1867); William Douglass, *A Summary, Historical and Political, of the First Planting, Progressive Improvements, and Present State of the British Settlements in North-America*, 2 vols. (London: R. and J. Didsley, 1760); James P. Baxter, ed., *Documentary History of the State of Maine*, 16 vols. (Portland: Lefavor-Tower Co., 1907–1916). See also Douglas R. McManis, *European Impressions of the New England Coast, 1497–1620* (University of Chicago Department of Geography Research Paper no. 139); Richard Arthur Preston, *Gorges of Plymouth Fort* (Toronto: University of Toronto Press, 1953); and Bernard Bailyn, *The New England Merchants in the Seventeenth Century* (Cambridge: Harvard University Press, 1979). I also relied heavily on the appendix of Belknap's *History of New-Hampshire*, in which he included copies of correspondence and other documents illustrative of these matters. Based on hints in Penhallow's *Indian Wars* as well as other sources (such as Myron O. Stachiw, *Massachusetts Officers and Soldiers, 1723–1743, Dummers War to the War of Jenkins' Ear.* Boston: Society of Colonial Wars, 1979), "Captain Wells" may very well have been Captain Thomas Wells of Deerfield, Massachusetts.

For a good description of the species of flora and fauna of the White Mountains see Frederic L. Steele, *At Timberline: A Nature Guide to the Mountains of the Northeast* (Boston: Appalachian Mountain Club, 1982). Fred Beckey, *Mountains of North America* (San Francisco: Sierra Club Books, 1982), provides a nice description of mountains of the Northeast. For a contemporary perspective of the Appalachian, "endless,"

Mountains, see Thomas Jefferson's "Notes on Virginia" in Adrienne Koch and William Peden, eds., *The Life and Selected Writings of Thomas Jefferson* (New York: Modern Library, 1944). Lawrence Martin, "Who Named Mountain Washington?" *The Geographical Review* 28(1938), provides a basic assessment of the problem.

For Washington's visit to Portsmouth see Edwin L. Page, *George Washington in New Hampshire* (Boston: Houghton Mifflin, 1932); the *New Hampshire Gazette*, November 5, 1789; Benson J. Lossing, ed., *The Diary of George Washington, from 1789 to 1791* (New York: Charles B. Richardson & Co., 1860); Charles W. Brewster, *Rambles About Portsmouth* (Portsmouth: C. W. Brewster & Son, 1859).

# Index